Researching your
FAMILY HISTORY

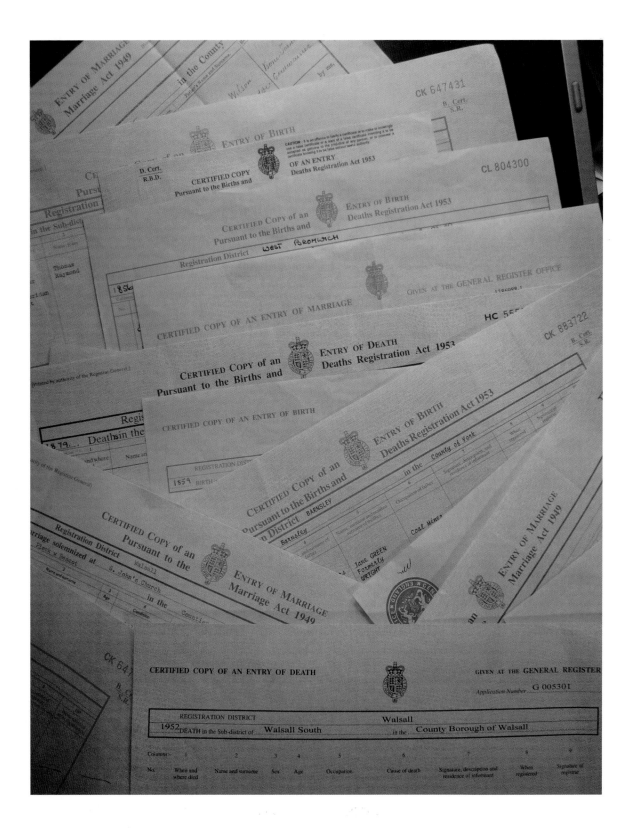

Researching your
FAMILY HISTORY

PAM ROSS

THE CROWOOD PRESS

First published in 2010 by
The Crowood Press Ltd
Ramsbury, Marlborough
Wiltshire SN8 2HR

www.crowood.com

British Library Cataloguing-in-Publication Data
A catalogue record for this book is available from the British Library.

ISBN 978 1 84797 209 5

Frontispiece: Certificates Crown Copyright. Photo: Tom Ross

Typeset by Phoenix Typesetting, Auldgirth, Dumfriesshire
Printed and bound in Malaysia by Times Offset (M) Sdn Bhd

Contents

Dedication

For Tom, David and Kenneth

Acknowledgements

Many thanks are due to Ann Ash and Doreen Hopwood for reading and suggesting improvements; and to Tom Ross for reading and asking all the right questions. Also to Karen Bali, Hilary Berry, Mr and Mrs F D Muntz, Wendy Sugden, Dr David Wykes and John Yates. And collectively to the ever-helpful staff at the Birmingham Library and Archives, Birmingham Register Office, the Bodleian Library, Oxford and the Internet Library of Early Journals, Lichfield Diocesan Record Office, London Metropolitan Archives, the National Archives, the National Army Museum, Staffordshire Record Office, the National Library of Wales and Walsall Local History Centre. Thanks also to Trinity Mirror PLC; the Rector and Churchwardens of St Martin, Birmingham and of St Swithun's, Shobrooke; the Vicar and Churchwardens of All Saints, Alrewas, and of St Mary Magdalene, Tanworth in Arden; the Moravian Church in Great Britain and Ireland; the Staffordshire Parish Registers Society; the Tanworth in Arden Branch of the Royal British Legion, Veterans UK; and my extended family – past and present.

Any errors or omissions are mine.

Introduction

This is intended to be the kind of book I would have wanted when I first started researching my own family history. The task facing new researchers has altered since then. In just a few years, because of the increase in use of the internet, family history has gone from being an obscure hobby to a big business aimed at as many customers as it can attract.

At the same time there has been a transformation in the way research is done. Many of the documents that researchers used to view in original form or on a scratched piece of microfilm or microfiche are now available to people at home on a computer screen. There are services on offer that, for a monthly or annual fee, will bring 'thousands of names' and access to many images and indexes.

All very exciting, but it seems to detract from the fact that what people are looking for has not changed. In whatever way we eventually view it – electronically, on film or fiche or in its original form – we are going to be looking at a piece of paper or parchment which has been written mainly by administrators or clerks who, like the rest of us, sometimes made mistakes in their work.

The aim of this book is to concentrate on those pieces of paper and to help new researchers to understand what they are looking for and looking at – and why it could help in their search. And by focusing on some of those sources most likely to suggest family relationships, my hope is that it will then help beginners to make informed and economical choices when it comes to gaining access to the images of the documents that will help to prove a family tree.

I have concentrated on research in England and Wales going back roughly to the introduction of parish registers during the reign of Elizabeth I; a span of several hundred years – which will occupy most researchers for

What do I look for?

The type of document you are going to be looking for varies depending on the period of time you are covering in your search.

As a rough guide:

1911 to present: Family memories and papers; birth, marriage and death certificates; parish registers; directories; newspapers and magazines; armed services records; monumental inscriptions and cemetery records; wills and administrations.

1837 to 1911: Census returns (these are only available 100 years after the information was collected); birth, marriage and death certificates; parish registers; directories; newspapers; institutional records; armed services records; monumental inscriptions and cemetery records; wills and administrations; solicitors' collections; early family papers.

1538 to 1837: Parish registers; parish chest; wills and administrations; local censuses; manorial records; solicitors' collections; early family papers. From the late eighteenth century a few early directories and newspapers. Monumental inscriptions from the late seventeenth century; army and navy records; printed and manuscript family trees.

The list above is not exhaustive but it will get you off to a good start if you use it along with the information in the following chapters. Question every source, even those that look impressive and official, and back up your findings with other information from other sources.

some time! There is some common ground for people searching in Scotland and Ireland but there are books written specifically with Scottish and Irish research in mind listed at the back of the book. For people whose families are relatively recent arrivals in England or Wales, or whose families left some time ago, this book should help with documents covering their time here, but there are specialist publications covering research overseas. In a book of this size there is not the space to do justice to these areas of research.

'I HAVE RESEARCHED MY FAMILY TREE BACK TO 1066 – ALL ON THE INTERNET!'

All of us have heard this said, at one time or another. It is perfectly possible to get a very nice family tree by researching entirely on the internet – however, the chances of it all being your own family tree are a bit remote! Even today, when images of more and more original documents are being made available online, your choice of where to research next should be guided by what is needed and not what is easily available. Once you have made good use of the excellent resources now available online – get out of your swivel chair and make for the archives.

Finally, pause occasionally as you make your search. These documents you are looking for are important – not only for the information they can give you but also for the moment in time they represent – the point in your family's history when they were written, read through and signed. Don't forget to enjoy that too.

Look around for things that will tell you where people were, and when. (Photos: P.M. Jones and Tom Ross.)

1 How Do I Start?

THE BASIC METHOD

Always start with what you and your family think they know as 'fact' and work backwards using official documents, and personal papers if you have them. Official documents are your proof that an event actually happened and that people are related, but it is up to you to put together the evidence as soundly and thoroughly as if your most severe critic were going to cross-examine you on it later. You do this by looking at your first piece of evidence, perhaps your own birth certificate, and checking it against what else you know. Note any differences or inconsistencies so you can check them out. Note any similarities and use these to build up your body of evidence as you collect more and more documents.

One generation at a time
Then just work backwards, step by step, noting what you have found and also every reference number for every document. Your birth certificate will contain the name of at least one parent, so already you have taken your story back one generation (see Chapter 2 for more ideas). Also, keep looking sideways at every stage – particularly at brothers and sisters.

A useful tip
The more you know about your wider family the less likely you are to get lost. For example, you might find you have lost the trail of Fred SMITH. You can't find a record of his birth anywhere. You know that Fred had a brother Thomas SMITH who was in the army. A search for Thomas's army attestation papers (see Chapter 9) might give you at least a date and place of birth for Thomas. By following up the details on Thomas you might find where and when he was born or baptized, and the names of his parents. With luck this information might help to lead you to details of Fred. (Also don't forget that even a simple name like Smith had a lot of possible spellings – Smith, Smithe, Smyth, Smythe and so on.)

Where there's a will...
Perhaps Fred had a younger sister who never married. When she died she might have left a will, leaving items to members of the wider family (see Chapter 5). The names you find in the will might give you names of some other family members you had never heard of. More people to follow up in order to take your family tree back another generation with confidence.

Background information
Your basic aim should be to find details of where and when your individual ancestor was born, married and died. But family history is more than just a list of names with a series of three dates. You should try to find out as much about the national and local history surrounding your ancestors' lives as you can because, apart from the fact that the research brings life to the cold facts, the more you know the less likely you are to make a mistake going backwards to the next generation. For example, if you find out your ancestor worked on the railways, that gives you a whole new set of work-related records to look for. And the more you know about the history of the railways, and how people progressed in their employment – from cleaning the engines to driving them, for example – the better you will be able to understand the records you are searching. Apart from the fact that it is a great way to learn more about history in general, the chances are that this knowledge will stand you in very good stead if you hit a sticking point later in your research.

There is no single source to go to for all the

information on your family's history. Perhaps the first thing to understand about the spread of archives across the country is that there was no Master Plan. Documents ended up in one place or the other for administrative reasons to do with the Church or Government – not in order to help us with our family history. Many will be missing or not available because of privacy laws. Some can be searched for online but many will have to be visited where they are – in local, county and national archives up and down the country.

ASK THE FAMILY

Much of what is known already is in the collective memories of your own family. First of all write down what you know yourself and where you think the infor-

Twentieth-century research

You would think that, being in the recent past, the twentieth century would be easy to research but it is often quite difficult. Privacy laws mean that many records, such as census returns after 1911, are not yet open to be viewed by the public. This is one of the reasons why the information you obtain from your own family can make all the difference.

mation came from. Then ask other family members what they know, being careful not to ask leading questions. Take every opportunity to chat, particularly to older members, but ask your own contemporaries too because different members of the family are told different things.

Old family documents are useful to give you a date, a place or a name. (Photo: Tom Ross)

Even if they were part of the same conversation they never remember things in an identical way (in other circumstances the basis of many a family argument!). And make sure you write it down. You will never remember it all.

Varying layers of knowledge are passed on or remembered. If there is a big age gap, in particular, the older siblings will have lived through more of the family's history and picked up different stories in passing. Ask to see family photos and ask their owners to write on the back the names of the people in them. Ask if there are still birth, marriage or death certificates in the family – or certificates of baptism. Also, don't forget to ask if they know of anyone in the family who has already done some work on the family tree.

Be tactful and patient. Also, be aware that there might be family stories that you will never be told. Family secrets are often buried deep. If they are going to come out it will probably not be while anyone is alive who could be hurt by them. So if you find something in your research that doesn't add up, tread very carefully if you ask a family member about it. Simply write down the details that emerge from any odd or strained conversations. All might become clear at a later date. The gentler you are in asking the questions the more likely you are to get an answer that is useful to you in your research.

'Oh, didn't you know about Aunt Bessie...?

Another point about family secrets is that they are not always secret in all branches of the family. Another part of the family might talk about it openly, so spread the net as wide as you can and let people talk.

What do I need to know?

Who? Where? When? You need to gather information about dates or years of birth, names and relationships. If they can't remember all the names, ask how many boys and how many girls, did they have nicknames or middle names, when they were born, where did they live? Did they always live there? Did they speak with an accent? What kind of jobs did they do? Did they change jobs? When did they die? (Even a rough idea would be helpful.) Where did they die? (Even the name of a town or county will lead to further information.) Any idea where they

were buried? (People can sometimes remember visiting family graves as children.) Did they do military service? Did they attend a church? What school did they go to? When did they marry? Again, a rough idea can be very helpful. Where did they marry? Were they married more than once? You need to find out married names and maiden names. Perhaps, above all, who else should you talk to? Write it all down as soon as you can – preferably while you are talking. Some people find it helpful to make up a 'form' that includes some of these questions and fill it in while they chat.

GETTING THE FAMILY TO TALK

Many researchers are very keen on digital or tape recording of conversations – perhaps alongside a look through family photos. Think carefully about this before you do it, and make a judgement on its possible advantages and disadvantages with regard to each individual you are going to talk to. Although it is good to have someone's voice to listen to, recording will not always work for everyone. Will the person you are going to interview be put off by the microphone, for example? You might find that you do not get all the facts if people think it is being recorded; just as journalists get their best stories off the record, then so do family historians. Would you, perhaps, be better off sometimes in an informal setting with a notebook 'to make a note of the names'? A lot of the best information emerges after a couple of glasses of wine at Christmas over the washing up. Be prepared for a soggy notebook! And be prepared to spend some time transcribing a recording or putting what you have been told into readable note form.

One very important point – if someone from your family supplies you with a copy of research they have already done, be careful how you use it. If you would like to publish the information online or in book form then ask their permission first. And if you do publish it, make sure you acknowledge where it has come from.

What family documents should I look for?

As well as the more obvious things like photographs, and birth, marriage and death certificates, look for birthday books, ration books, bank books, old letters and cards, postcards and old diaries – even just appointment diaries. These can give you an idea of where people were,

Identity cards can give you changes of name and address.

and when. Take a note of addresses and of the dates people are shown as being at these addresses. The date on a postcard addressed to an ancestor can be a valuable clue to the fact that they were living at that particular address at that time, even if what is written on the card might remain a mystery. Birthday books can be a particular help. Even if the year of birth is not written down, knowing the day and the month can cut down the amount of work you have to do to find a copy of a birth certificate. Make sure you read any old, faded newspaper cuttings from the backs of drawers – they were all kept for a reason.

You might come across some family stories that sound a bit far-fetched, but make a note of them anyway because there is probably some truth to be found in them. A story that is often used as an example is of the well-remembered ancestor who had a close acquaintance with the Duke of Wellington. This was duly noted and explored and eventually a connection was found – the Duke of Wellington was the name of his much-visited local pub! Whether the story is true or not, it is a good example of the kind of 'sideways' thinking you need to do to be a successful family historian.

PHOTOGRAPHS

Make a resolution that, from today, you will always label your family photos with a name, a place and a date. We know who the people in them are now but someone coming along later will not have a clue. Similarly, our attics are full of old photographs that no-one can identify. Several good books and articles have been written about how to date old photographs by the clothes that people are wearing and even the way the photos are staged. Jayne Shrimpton's *Family Photographs & How to Date Them* and Neil Storey's *Military Photographs & How to Date Them* are just two.

PLAN YOUR RESEARCH

A big challenge lies in keeping the budget for your family history research as low as possible without compromising the outcome. Buying copies of documents costs money, and travelling expenses to visit archives and libraries also have to be taken into account.

Many people want to search for their family's story. Few have much time or money to devote to it, so it is important that the time and money you do spend on it is focused and planned.

Unfortunately one of the most expensive parts comes first – the purchase of copies of birth, marriage and death certificates for the information they contain (*see* Chapter 2). It is a good idea, for the sake of economy, to

Some golden rules

- If you borrow photographs to copy, return them within days rather than weeks.
- If you write to a distant member of the family, enclose a stamped, self-addressed envelope (you are more likely to get a reply that way).
- If you email someone you don't know well, make sure you identify yourself in the heading and start the email with some information about yourself so that they don't think it is a 'phishing' email.
- Tell people who have helped you if you find out anything that might interest them.
- Don't assume that everyone is as interested in your family's history as you are.

decide which of your parents' or grandparents' family names you would like to follow first – perhaps the least common name or the side of the family you know most about already – and put your money and your effort into doing that one branch well.

Always be prepared to change your mind if you hit a dead end. Ways of searching around a problem are discussed later but if you have tried these with no luck remember that there are plenty of branches to this tree you are investigating. It is often helpful to leave a difficult problem to one side and come back to it later with more experience and fresh eyes.

WHAT IF I HAVE NO FAMILY AROUND TO ASK?

Start with what you know about yourself and work backwards. With luck, you should at least have your own birth certificate, or be able to obtain a copy (see Chapter 2). That should contain at least one of your parents' names and occupation. If there are two names, follow the advice in the next chapter about looking for a marriage certificate. If you have only a death certificate for one or other of your parents, then that should give you an age at death from which to work out roughly when they were born. Then follow the advice in the next chapter about finding a birth certificate.

Search your memory for lost conversations and names, and revisit places that seemed important when you were a child. Did you ever go to visit the grave of a family member? Ask family friends or anyone from your parents' past what they knew. If all else fails, seek professional help at least for the initial stages of your search. If you have had contact with social services during your childhood they might be able to offer some information. Some of the advice in the following section on Adoption might also be helpful. Don't be put off. Because a thing is difficult does not mean that it is impossible.

ADOPTION

You might be reading this from the position of not knowing who your natural parents were. If that is the case there are now procedures in place whereby you can apply to find out this information and get help and support along the way. The Charity NORCAP specializes in helping Adults Affected by Adoption, including both adopted adults and birth and adoptive parents. Try their website or write to them (see Further Information). There are also professional researchers, members of the Association of Genealogists and Researchers in Archives who offer adoption searches. The British Association for Adoption and Fostering also has a website, a section of which aims to be a first port of call for people seeking more information about their early life. Look out for an article by Karen Bali in *Your Family Tree* magazine issue 64 (May 2008) for more detailed advice.

Once you have found out who your natural parents were you will then be in a position to look into your family history using the information you have – irrespective of whether you want to try to make contact with surviving relatives. If you do decide to look for living relatives, don't attempt it on your own – let yourself be guided by the professionals. Remember always that raw feelings can be aroused by this kind of search – not only in your adoptive family but also in the family that gave you up for adoption in the first place. Memories are long and strong feelings can be passed down through the generations, so try to keep an open mind if you decide to look for surviving family members.

History of adoption

Adoption became a formal procedure in England and Wales from 1927. If you or any member of your family was adopted after this time you should be able to apply to the General Register Office at Southport for a copy of their certificate of adoption as long as they are over 18. The information on this certificate is sparse but if you are the person adopted you should be able to proceed to an application for your birth certificate and find out the information you are looking for with the help of the agencies mentioned above. If you are looking for information on a family member who was adopted after 1927 there is a limit to the amount of information you can be given by government departments.

Before 1927 adoption was often informal. Family members would take in a child from the extended family, or even the immediate neighbourhood, and raise it as their own without anything being written on paper. In most cases you might never know this has taken place except perhaps if it is mentioned in a will or a letter. The

Guardians of the Poor who ran the Union Workhouses or, before them, the Parish Overseers of the Poor might have arranged adoptions for pauper children, or boarded or apprenticed them with local families. If records survive, there might be a mention in the poor law documents of the parish (see Chapter 8) or in the records of the local Poor Law Union.

Some adoptions were arranged privately. Any records of this happening would be hard to find but might survive in solicitors' papers. Some nineteenth-century charities who looked after orphaned children also arranged adoptions so there might be records in their archives.

WHAT HAVE OTHER PEOPLE FOUND ALREADY?

The Guild of One-Name Studies

You might be lucky enough to find that a name you are interested in has been registered with the Guild of One-Name Studies. The Guild is a charitable organization with a world-wide reach dedicated to helping those interested in a particular surname to co-ordinate their efforts in finding examples of their name of interest and its variants. There is a list of registered surnames on their website, or you could write, enclosing a stamped self-addressed envelope. All those involved are volunteers, so be patient if you do not get a reply straight away.

Marshall, Whitmore, Barrow and Thomson

These dedicated genealogists spent many hours trawling through published versions of family trees containing more than three generations and extracting the surnames mentioned in them. The result is four publications that give details of the surnames extracted and where the relevant family tree is to be found. Copies can usually be found in public libraries, archives and the library of the Society of Genealogists. They are particularly useful for early research and for less common names. For common names you really need to have an idea of location in order to benefit fully from their efforts. Every time you come across a new name that is of interest to you it is worth making a note to consult these books the next time you are in a library.

Burke's Peerage and Debrett's Peerage

Few people have not heard of Burke's and Debrett's. The 'pedigrees' or family trees they list are relevant to many of us – even if they simply refer to families for whom our ancestors worked. It is more possible than you might think to find a link with an apparently ordinary family. Younger sons and daughters of aristocrats and gentry did not always marry into their own class.

Don't be tempted, however, to assume that you are descended from a particular aristocratic family and work down the generations from their family tree in the hope of it joining up with yours somewhere. Always work backwards from what you know, and if you are fortunate enough to find a link then books such as Burke's and Debrett's will come into their own. Copies of both are available at libraries and archives. Look out also for Burke's Landed Gentry and Burke's Dormant and Extinct Peerages and Cockayne's Complete Peerage.

Heralds' visitations

During the sixteenth and seventeenth centuries checks were made every thirty years or so on whether people who used Coats of Arms were entitled to bear them. The Heralds, representing the Monarch, noted down the evidence people gave about their family tree and would often include a pedigree. Many of their findings have been published (you can find them in libraries and archives) and some of the names included in books such as Whitmore's.

Manuscript pedigrees

Many county archives hold manuscript 'pedigrees' or family trees, and printed versions of pedigrees, relevant to families in their own county. The Society of Genealogists has a collection of manuscript pedigrees. The National Library of Wales holds some pedigree rolls from fifteenth to twentieth centuries in its General Manuscripts' collection. The British Library catalogue shows both printed and manuscript pedigrees.

Lists of interests

Wherever you go – online, in person or as a member of a Family History Society – it is likely that you will find a register of interests with names and contact details of people interested in finding others who are researching

SIDMOUTH.

HENRY ADDINGTON, Viscount **SIDMOUTH,** of Sidmouth, co. Devon, P.C. High Steward of Westminster and Reading, Governor of the Charter House, an Elder Brother of the Trinity House, Deputy Ranger of Richmond Park, F.S.A. and D.C.L.; late Recorder of Devizes, sometime Secretary of State for the Home Department; *born* 1757; *married* Ursula-Mary, da. and co-h. of Leonard Hammond, of Cheam, co. Surrey, esq. son of William Hammond, esq. sometime representative in parliament for the borough of Southwark, and by her (who *d.* 23 June 1811) had issue,—— 1. HENRY, clerk of the pells in the exchequer, *b.* 1787, *d. unm.* 30 July 1823;——2. WILLIAM-LEONARD, in holy orders, rector of Poole, co. Wilts, *m.* 20 April 1820, Mary, da. of the rev. John Young, rector of Thorpe, co. Northampton, and has issue, 1. *Mary-Ursula, b.* 4 Feb. 1821, *m.* 15 April 1841, M. C. Seton, esq.; 2. *Henry, b.* 17 Feb. 1823; 3. *William, b.* May 1825; 4. *Louisa;* 5. a *son, b.* 4 April 1830; 6. a *da. b.* 18 Sept. 1839;——3. MARY-ANNE;——4. FRANCES, *m.* 29 June 1820, the hon. and rev. George Pellew, dean of Norwich, and prebendary of York, 3d son of Edward, 1st viscount Exmouth, G.C.B.;——5. CHARLOTTE, *m.* 2 May 1838, the rev. Horace Gore Currie;——6. HENRIETTA, *b.* 17 June 1800, *m.* 16 Jan. 1838, Thomas Barker Wall, esq. His lordship *m.* 2dly, 29 July 1823, Marianne, da. and sole h. of William Scott, lord Stowell, elder brother of the earl of Eldon, and widow of Thomas Townshend, of Honington Hall, co. Warwick, esq.

ARMS—Per pale, ermine and ermines, a chevron charged with five lozenges, counterchanged between three fleurs-de-lis or. CREST—A cat-a-mountain sejant guardant proper, semée of bezants, and the dexter fore paw resting on an escocheon azure, charged with a mace erect or, within a border engrailed argent. SUPPORTERS—Two stags, the *dexter* ermines, the *sinister* ermine, both attired and gorged with a chain, therefrom pendent a key or. MOTTO—" Libertas sub rege pio." Liberty under a pious king.

ANTHONY ADDINGTON, of Trinity College, Oxford, M.D. *b.* 13 Dec. 1713, *m.* 22 Sept. 1745, Mary, da. of Haviland-John Hiley, clerk, and by her (who *d.* 7 Nov. 1778) had issue,

1. HENRY, present viscount Sidmouth.
2. Right hon. JOHN-HILEY, of Longford, co. Somerset, *d.* 11 June 1818, having *m.* 25 Oct. 1785, Mary, da. of Henry Unwin, esq. by whom (who *d.* 3 Sept. 1833) he had issue,
   1. Haviland-John, *b.* 20 Nov. 1787.
   2. Henry-Unwin, late envoy extraordinary and minister plenipotentiary at the court of Spain, *b.* 24 March 1790.
   3. Mary, *b.* 31 Dec. 1788.
3. ANNE, *m.* 2 June 1770, William Goodenough, of Oxford, M.D. *d.* 12 June 1806.
4. ELEANOR, *m.* 1 Aug. 1771, James Sutton, of New Park, near Devizes, esq. and *d.* 21 Jan. 1837.
5. ELIZABETH, *m.* William Hoskins, of South Perrot, co. Somerset, esq. and *d.* his widow 26 June 1827.
6. CHARLOTTE, *m.* 1 Aug. 1788, the right hon. Charles Bragge, of Lydney Park, co. Gloucester, sometime chancellor of the duchy of Lancaster, and president of the board of control for the affairs of India; who obtained his majesty's royal licence and authority, 11 May 1804, that he and his issue may assume and take the surname and bear the arms of *Bathurst* only; she *d.* his widow 27 May 1839.

Heir Apparent—Hon. WILLIAM-LEONARD ADDINGTON, his lordship's eldest surviving son. *Creation*—12 Jan. 1805.

A page from *Debrett's Peerage of Great Britain and Ireland 1841*. (By kind agreement of Debretts.)

the same surname in your area. Even if you don't find anyone, if you add your name to the list you can then be contacted. The names and web addresses of the most popular sites might change from time to time but GENUKI lists the more prominent ones in its introductory pages.

LOCAL HISTORY

Many local history books will contain family trees of prominent families in the area. An interest in the history of the area you are researching is vital in any case, so keep a look out for anything that might be relevant. Also, familiarize yourself with the *Victoria County History* series. It relates only to England and does not cover all areas of all counties because it is still a work in progress but, where complete, is invaluable as a knowledgeable guide to most aspects of a county's history. Information on prominent families is likely to be included, as are details on the formation of towns, villages and churches. The part relating to Walsall in Staffordshire, for example, has sections on The Growth of the Town, Communications, Manors, Other Estates, Economic History, Local Government, Public Services and Parliamentary History. There are notes on the history of individual Churches, Roman Catholicism, Protestant non-conformity, Non-Christian Religions, Social Life, Education and Charities for the Poor [*VCH Staffordshire, Volume 17*]. *VCH* is available in most large libraries and is now also being published online at British History Online.

Where to next?

Once you have gathered together as much information as you can from the sources described in this chapter, and as many family copies of birth, marriage and death certificates as you can, you should find yourself a good filing system and then move forward with your search. The early stages of research are laid out in the chapters following this one. Different methods of filing the paper information are discussed in Chapter 12.

Do I have to sign up to an online family history website to search?

No, although if you have the internet available at home you might want to consider it, at least for a period of time.

What if I have no internet connection at home?

It is possible to do research into your family history without an internet connection at home. Before the advent of computers, people searched at their local library or archive using original documents and microfilm or microfiche copies of them. That option is still available to you in most places. It is possible that they will have microfiche copies of the General Register Office indexes to births, marriages and deaths although these are not held by everyone, or for all dates (*see* Chapter 2) and also census returns for their area (*see* Chapter 4), plus microfilm or fiche copies of local parish registers. Call and ask them if they have the years you are looking for. There are printed versions of some census indexes, particularly 1851, in many libraries and also printed transcripts of some parish registers.

Local libraries and archives also have computers with connections to the internet available (usually you need to book) and you can use them to follow the advice given in this book. Some have arrangements with specific family history providers to give you free access to their service so it is worth phoning round the libraries and archives in your area to see what they have available.

If you are able to visit the National Archives at Kew you can access free of charge all their documents that have been digitally reproduced online. It costs you nothing to look. If you want a copy then it will cost you a few pence to print one off. This is very useful if you are looking for wills because you can read them through before you decide to buy.

The Family History Centres around the country run by the Church of Jesus Christ of Latter-day Saints (LDS, also

Online security

If you are tempted to pay for a service or buy a copy of an image online by credit card, especially when using a computer in a public place, do take sensible precautions to protect your personal details. Look for the padlock symbol on the website but if you have any doubts about security, don't do it. There is highly likely to be another way of paying if you look for it. Or another way of getting at the information you want.

known as the Mormons) are particularly useful if you have no computer. They can often order an item for you from their library in Utah if they do not have it available. You can find details of the centre nearest to you either by phoning your nearest Mormon Church or looking online at the Familysearch website (see Further Information).

The library at the Society of Genealogists in London has a vast stock of books, microfilm and microfiche and also access via their own computers to many of the things that are available online. There is still a lot you can do without a computer at home.

Another alternative, if you do have a computer but no internet connection, is to look at the provision on compact disk of census and parish register material. S & N Genealogy Supplies has long been active in this field and a lot of family history societies produce their own material on CD. Libraries and archives are likely to have collected some of those CDs relevant to their own area.

Which online family history website should I choose?

A difficult question because they keep adding to their collections. The first thing to do is to note how many things are available on the internet completely free of charge.

SOME OF THE MOST USEFUL FREE WEBSITES

For full details of the following websites please see the list at the back of the book:

- *FreeBMD* is an electronic index to the pages of the quarterly General Register Office indexes. It covers most of the nineteenth and the early twentieth century, with access to some images of the original pages.
- *FreeCEN* is an electronic index to the nineteenth century census returns. Some counties are complete and there is a clear guide, county by county as to what has been indexed.
- *FreeREG* is a growing database of transcribed parish registers.
- *Familysearch* (includes a large number of parish registers and an index to the 1881 census). A long-established worldwide database of parish registers

including the International Genealogical Index. Run by the Church of Jesus Christ of Latter Day Saints.
- *Historical Directories* is a digital library of eighteenth, nineteenth and early twentieth century trades directories. Search by location, decade or key words.
- *Internet Library of Early Journals* – digital scans of eighteenth and nineteenth century journals including *Gentleman's Magazine 1731 to 1750*.
- *GENUKI* – a free website, run by volunteers, which aims to be a 'virtual reference library' mainly leading to primary sources for family history research. The information, for the UK and Ireland, is presented under headings for each county. GENUKI is a registered charity run in conjunction with the Federation of Family History Societies and its member societies.
- *Cyndi's List* – an American-based site with a massive number of links to genealogical websites all over the world.
- *Victoria County Histories* at British History Online.
- The National Library of Wales *Welsh Wills Online* gives the opportunity to view free over 190,000 Welsh wills. Only copies have to be paid for.
- Gazettes Online – *The London Gazette*, *The Edinburgh Gazette* and *The Belfast Gazette*.

THE MAIN COMMERCIAL ONLINE PROVIDERS

These are as follows:

- Ancestry
- Findmypast
- GenesReunited
- Origins Network
- The Genealogist
- Documents Online is the National Archives' service providing digital images of some of the documents in its collection, including wills.
- BMD Registers provides images of non-conformist registers from the National Archives
  (See Further Information for details of all these websites.)

How do I choose?

This is a little bit like trying to hit a moving target because the commercial sites seem to change daily. You can keep abreast of some of the changes by reading the computer

Things to consider when making a choice of an online family history website

- Take advantage of free trial offers and give their system a thorough workout.
- Do you find their search engine easy to use? You can lose a lot of time making frustrating mistakes.
- How accurate is their search engine?*
- Do they publish the documents you want to see? Check the availability and coverage of census returns from 1841 to 1911, for example.
- Do they have an agreement with a particular archive to publish items that will be of use to you? For example Ancestry has an arrangement with the London Metropolitan Archives.
- Are they offering digital images or just an index?
- Try to do a cost comparison by comparing the different types of membership available.
- Remember that you do not have to stay with one provider indefinitely. See if they offer pay-per-view if you only want a little information – although the charges can stack up.

- Some will offer short-term membership. If they offer credits, check whether there is an expiry date and how generous it is.
- Documents from the National Archives at Kew, London that are offered online by various providers will be available to view via computer terminals at Kew free of charge. You can print copies while you are there.
- Check out whether you can find what you are looking for via the free sites listed above.
- Your local library or archives might have signed up to provide free access to at least one commercial site. Check whether it is one you are interested in and give it a try first.

*Some excellent articles have appeared in the family history magazines comparing the accuracy of the search engines of the online providers. Every few months one of the online experts gives the search engines another 'workout' and writes up their findings. Look through the magazine indexes to find the most up to date articles on the subject.

and internet articles in the family history magazines such as *Family Tree* or *Your Family Tree*. They will also tell you about any new free sites.

Have a look at all the sites. Many of them offer free trials or short-term membership and it is well worth making use of these. Also, membership of the Society of Genealogists gives you free access once a quarter to the Society's documents published online at Origins Network.

It is a good idea to review the situation over time because as you get further back in your research you might find that a particular provider has better coverage of the area you are interested in. Sign up for their newsletters so you can hear about any new additions that might change your priorities.

Although it may be tempting, try to resist becoming tied to the internet. There are a lot of records that have not been indexed and put online. You can find information about these in books, in the extensive

catalogues of county and national archives (these are now also largely online), by regular reading of the family history magazines or through your local family history society.

DNA

Many people believe that a study of DNA is the way forward for Family History.

The Guild of One-Name Studies has taken a particular interest in DNA studies because of their interest in looking at people who have held a particular surname. They have a website (*see* Further Information) and they are present at many of the Family History Fairs held around the United Kingdom. The Institute of Heraldic and Genealogical Studies (IHGS) has links via its website to a company that specialises in DNA for the purposes of Family History. There is an explanation of how it can be used for the purpose of identifying people who share the same ancestors and what the process of giving a sample

Do I need a computer program to store the information I find?

There is a discussion of ways of filing paper information in Chapter 12 but this seems a good place to discuss briefly whether a computer program is a good idea. There are a lot on the market, and their names and content change all the time.

- You do not need to buy a program straight away. It is probably a good idea to learn a bit about the 'mechanics' of collecting and writing up the information first. You will then be in more of a position to know which one will suit you.
- If you are tempted to get one, do some serious reading of people's opinions, both online and in the family history magazines. See what other people think of them and then look around and think which will be most useful to you. Ask other people and, if you have a friend or relative who uses one, ask if you can visit them and try it out or discuss with them what they like about it. Go and browse the boxes on the shelves of your local computer store.
- If you want to draw trees with your program look very carefully at what is on offer. You might want the capacity to move names and events around your tree with a certain amount of flexibility. You might want to put as many people on a page as you can for ease of reference. If this is the case avoid anything offering a set form with only three or four generations able to fit onto a page of A4 paper.
- You might want to look at how easy it might be to add new names to the tree, and how quickly the information you add can be absorbed into the database. Look carefully at the notes on how what you add can be retrieved. Will it be in a form that will fit in with your own style of note-taking?
- Most programs offer GEDCOM – Genealogical Data Communication – as part of the package. This is useful if you want to transfer your information to another person using a different program.
- It is highly probable that the basic version of any family tree program will be enough for most people. Once you learn more you can always upgrade and transfer the information you have already put in.
- Some online commercial providers such as those listed above offer the opportunity to store your information with them online. If you choose to go down this route, remember to keep a copy of everything at home as well.

of your DNA involves. The process of testing is not cheap and it is important to select the right family member for testing, depending on the result you are looking for.

Because DNA testing for this purpose is still in its infancy you might be tested and only receive an inconclusive answer about your origins. It all depends on who else has been interested enough to be tested already. At a time when more and more personal information is known about us by both the government and commercial companies it is a good idea to check very carefully the credentials of any company which offers testing of your DNA. For further reading try A. Savin's *A DNA For Family Historians* and the more recent *Family History in the Genes* by Chris Pomery.

Page 211

Marriage solemnized at The Parish Church in the Parish of Rye in the County of Sussex

No.	When Married.	Name and Surname.	Age.	Condition.	Rank or Profession.	Residence at the time of Marriage.	Father's Name and Surname.	Rank or Profession of Father.
122	July 19 1899	Walter Foster	23	Bachelor	Boilermaker	10 Tower St, Rye	James Foster (deceased)	Master Mariner
		Margaret Sultur	27	Spinster	—	(deceased) corner of 12 Alfred George Sultur	Alfred George Sultur	Fisherman

Married in the Parish Church according to the Rites and Ceremonies of the Established Church, after Banns, by me, Neville C. Bennett

This Marriage was solemnized between us, { Walter Foster, Margaret Sultur }

in the presence of us, { Alfred Sultur, Louisa Jane Sultur }

I Certify, that the foregoing is a true Extract from the Register of Marriages belonging to The Parish Church in the Parish of Rye

Witness my hand this nineteenth day of July 18 99

Neville C. Bennett

Designation Incumbent Priest

* NOTE.—Strike out that which does not apply.

Waterlow and Sons Limited, Printers, London Wall, London.

An original marriage certificate from 1899. (Crown Copyright.)

2 Certificates of Birth, Marriage and Death

What do I need to know before I start looking for certificates?

Searching for certificates comes in two parts: searching the General Register Office index for the name of your ancestor and then deciding whether to buy the certificate either from the centralized GRO or from the local register office where the event was registered.

There is very little information in the indexes about what the certificate will contain. You only get to see the personal information about your ancestor by buying a copy. Much of what follows in this chapter is designed, where possible, to help you to avoid making an expensive mistake by buying the wrong certificate.

Why do I need these certificates if they are so expensive?

An individual certificate is not cheap. If you buy several, the cost can mount up. And if you make a mistake and buy the wrong one it can be very frustrating.

You do need them, however. Certificates of birth, marriage and death will be the backbone of your research for the nineteenth, twentieth and twenty-first centuries. You would think that research into the more recent events of the twentieth and twenty-first centuries would be easy but without good family information it can, in fact, be quite hard because some of the records available for the period are still closed to public scrutiny.

The latest available census was taken in 1911. From 1911 to the present, because there is no census information available, family memories and documents, electoral registers, wills, newspapers and the available records generated by the two World Wars (*see* Chapter 9) will be

important in providing the additional information you need to find out about your ancestors. Key to using these other records is the information provided on certificates of birth, marriage and death.

From 1841 to 1911 there is a lot more information readily available. You can combine the information that certificates contain with information from the census returns that were taken every ten years (*see* Chapter 4) to get a picture of your ancestor's family.

A BRIEF BACKGROUND

The first births, marriages and deaths to be registered in a nationally co-ordinated system for England and Wales were recorded in July 1837. Before that, the best records available that might give you at least some of the information you want are the Church of England registers of baptisms, marriages and burials, along with some Catholic and non-conformist registers (*see* Chapters 6 and 7). This applies to Wales as well as England.

Before 1837 proof of who you were, whether or when you were married and when someone was buried came, in the main, through the Church. A parish priest could be asked to provide written evidence of an entry in his registers.

PREPARATION

Unless your ancestor has a very unusual name you will need to approach the search armed with a rough idea of the 'where and when' (at least to within a few years) of the birth, marriage or death you are looking for. It is a big advantage to have the full names of both bride and groom when searching the indexes for a marriage.

How do I get them?

Copies of certificates of birth, marriage and death can be bought from the local Registrar in the Registration District where the event happened or from what is usually known as the General Register Office (GRO), in Southport, which now comes under the banner of the Home Office Identity and Passport Service. First you need to look at the General Register Office Indexes.

GRO INDEXES

Whoever you choose to approach to obtain your certified copy of the certificate, you will need to consult the General Register Office Indexes of Births, Marriages and

The best preparation for ordering a copy certificate

You should try to find the name of your ancestor in the General Register Office indexes and note the Year, the Quarter, the name of the Registration District and, although you will not always need them, the two sets of numbers. These make up what is known as the GRO reference number.

It is always useful to have a good idea of the name of the Registration District your ancestor might have lived in at the time, particularly if you are looking for a common name. The latest version of *Phillimore's Atlas and Index of Parish Registers* (ed. C. Humphery-Smith) lists Registration Districts in the back next to the name of each parish. The Institute of Heraldic and Genealogical Studies has drawn up three very useful maps which show the names and numbers of Registration Districts over three separate periods of time: 1837–51, 1852–1946 and 1946–1965. Copies are in many libraries and archives. From 1852, for example, the numbering 1–3 covers London and the Home Counties, 6 the West Midlands, 9–10 the North of England and 11 represents Wales. When you get practised at it, you can recognize the Registration Districts in the indexes just from the numbers.

If you have the surnames of both bride and groom you can do an easy check in the indexes to see if you have the right marriage. Once you have found one of the names, the groom for example, make a note of the Registration District and the number (for example, Chorlton 8a 927). Look then for the name of the bride. That should have exactly the same Registration District and number next to it. It shows at least that the two names are on the same page of the register. There will be other marriages on that page as well, but you would be unlucky to have hit on the wrong one.

Quarters

March Quarter	= January – February – March
June Quarter	= April – May – June
September Quarter	= July – August – September
December Quarter	= October – November – December

Be aware that the indexes relate to the quarter a birth or death was registered, not the quarter in which it took place; so it is quite possible that a birth or death would be registered during the quarter after it took place. This could affect the year you are looking for as well as the quarter, for example a birth on 29 December one year might not be registered until January the following year. So if you cannot find an event in the quarter or year you expect, try the following one.

When searching the GRO indexes for a year of birth calculated from a census return or other documents, start by giving yourself a margin of error of at least two years each side of the date you calculate.

If you think that your ancestor was born in the few years before the start of Civil Registration in July 1837, look for the births of younger brothers and sisters after that date. Their birth certificate would give their mother's maiden name. Armed with this information you should then be able to find the marriage in a parish register. If the marriage pre-dates the birth of your direct ancestor you can be fairly confident that you have found your ancestor's parents.

Deaths to find the date when the event was registered. These indexes, dating from 1 July 1837, were originated every quarter in book form until 1984. Since then they have been listed annually. For family history purposes you will, for the most part, be dealing with the quarterly indexes.

For each quarter these indexes show a list of names sorted alphabetically by surname and then by first and second names. For each person listed they give you the name of the Registration District in which the event was recorded and the GRO volume number and page number.

For example: Smith Fred Chorlton 8a 927

Where can I see the GRO indexes?

Pages from the General Register Office indexes are available online, for a fee, at some of the commercial websites such as BMDIndex, Ancestry and Findmypast (*see* Further Information). The full range of years can be seen on microfiche at some major libraries and archives around the country (details at the DirectGov website www.direct.gov.uk under a search for 'GRO' and 'family history'). When you use the FreeBMD electronic index there are also some free images of the actual GRO index accessed via a link on the site.

Some smaller libraries and archives might have some, but not all, years covered by the GRO indexes. A phone call should tell you whether they have copies of the indexes for the years you are looking for. You might have to book a microfiche reader. Others will have access to the commercial sites via their computer networks. Most will not charge for access but some might make a small charge. This is something you can ask when you make the call.

Births and deaths were registered directly with the local Registrar who then copied out his register every three months and sent the copy to the GRO. This gives you two places where you might obtain a copy. Marriages were recorded where the event took place, so in addition to the copies with the GRO and the local Registrar, you might also be able to obtain a copy of the original entry from the parish register if the marriage took place in church.

Most pages of the indexes are typewritten and fairly easy to read. Some of the earlier ones are handwritten and can be difficult to make out. If you have this problem

An Index to an Index

Until recent years it has been necessary, when searching for an event in the GRO indexes, to consult four parts of the Indexes for every year. A few years ago a group of volunteers got together to produce an invaluable online index to the quarterly GRO indexes, which can be found at the FreeBMD website. As the title suggests, there is no cost involved in searching the database.

Transcription is not yet complete but information on the coverage for each year can be consulted. If you are lucky enough to find your ancestor's name at FreeBMD you should go to the GRO indexes themselves to confirm the information before ordering a certificate. Some images from the original indexes are available at FreeBMD, by clicking on the 'spectacles' symbol. Otherwise, advice is given above on where to find other copies of the indexes. FreeBMD has a higher level of accuracy than many online indexes but this is a check well worth doing, and recommended by FreeBMD itself, because it does not take long and it can save you time later.

The information that is freely available in FreeBMD is also included in some online paid-for packages. The GRO is also undertaking its own indexing and digitization project to give online access to the indexes. You should find more information and details of any changes in ordering procedure on the GRO website.

it can be a good idea to look at pages each side of the one you want. They might be a little clearer and give you a sense of the handwriting and the context of the entry you are looking for.

How do I order a copy?

GENERAL REGISTER OFFICE

Ordering a certificate from the General Register Office has become much easier in recent years with the advent of online ordering. If you know exactly what you want, including the reference number from the GRO indexes, your order will progress much more quickly and you will be more certain of getting the correct certificate. The

GRO can process requests without a reference number but these take longer.

The basic cost can be found at the certificate ordering website of the Home Office, Identity and Passport Service www.direct.gov.uk/gro. For the same price you can order by post, using a printed form, or on the telephone.

A copy of a certificate from the GRO will generally be a digital scan of the transcript of the certificate they were originally sent by the local Registrar at the end of the quarter when the event took place. It will, therefore, be roughly contemporaneous with the event but will not contain original signatures.

THE LOCAL REGISTRAR

Many researchers are very keen on ordering from the local Registrar where the event took place. This is quite

easy to do and the certificates are slightly cheaper. The GRO index will have given you the name of a Registration District. It may not exist any longer but GENUKI, the freely accessible family history website should tell you which present-day Registrar is likely to hold copies of the registers you are looking for. *The Family and Local History Handbook,* available in libraries and many archives, has a list of names and addresses of Registrars for each county.

Many Register Offices now have websites where you can order online or download a form to send off with your payment. They will often ask for a stamped, self-addressed envelope. This can be to your advantage because you can send a large A4 envelope, with an appropriate large stamp, so that the certificate can be kept flat, whereas those ordered from the GRO come folded in an A5 envelope. You can also request your certificate by letter.

SAVE MONEY

Writing a letter has the advantage that you can send a cheque with your request and ask the Register Office to check small items for you before processing the payment. For example if you have two births of John Smith in the same Registration District, both in the quarter you are interested in, you can supply details of an address or the father's name or mother's maiden name to guide them to the correct certificate. Registrars do not generally charge for this kind of thing because it helps them to identify the correct certificate. If you ask them to do too complicated a search, for which they might have to charge, they will consult you before proceeding. If it can be established before issuing a certificate that it is not the correct one they should not usually charge anything at all, but do check this out. Register Offices are generally constrained from giving you any information at all from a certificate you do not purchase but they can let you know if any of the information you provide does not match.

The information they need is the name of the person or people you are looking for, the type of event (birth, marriage or death), the year in which it was registered and the quarter in which it was registered (March, June, September or December). Generally speaking, the GRO reference number is of little interest or use to a

Keep an eye on your budget

Copies of certificates of birth, marriage and death are probably the most expensive items you will need in tracing your family history. Unfortunately they also come at the beginning of the process of discovery. It is a good idea to check with family members in case there are still original certificates in the family because that would save you money. They might only have a short version of a birth certificate, however, which would not give you all the information you need. If you are not sure what kind you have, look at the full birth certificate shown on page 28 for a comparison.

If you are on a tight budget and cannot afford to buy a new certificate at any stage, it is a good idea to consider whether there might be any church records that might help. If you don't know which church they might have attended, wait a while and research the social history around your family or check online to see if anyone else is researching the same line.

If you type 'certificates of birth marriage and death' into a search engine it will come up with people offering to provide a service and get them for you at a flat rate, which is currently at least ten pounds more than the actual cost of the certificate because it includes a search fee. If you have all the details and know what you want there is no need to take up this particular offer.

Marriage certificates from Parish Registers

If a marriage took place in a Register Office your only options for obtaining a copy of the marriage certificate are to apply to the local Registrar or the GRO. If the marriage took place in a church, by far the cheapest way of obtaining a copy of a marriage certificate is to obtain a printout from the microfilm or microfiche copies of parish registers held by local libraries and archives. In order to do this, however, you do need to know the name of the church where the marriage took place. If you do not live close enough to the area to make the search yourself you also need to know the date of the marriage to avoid incurring search charges if you make a request for a printout by mail.

A couple of things to consider here:

- If it is important to you to see your ancestor's signature, perhaps to compare with other documents, and you cannot get a digitally scanned copy from the local registrar, you could use the information on the certificate they or the GRO provide to request a parish register printout from a library or archive.
- If you live at a distance from the area where the marriage took place – some local family history societies will offer to swap effort with you and might do a search or make a copy if you will return the favour, for one of their members, in a library or record office near where you live.

local Registrar. Ask them or consult their website if you are in any doubt. Include a phone number where they can contact you during office hours in case of any queries.

Some Register Offices have digital scanning equipment so the copy certificate they provide will, if possible, be an image of the original, sometimes including your ancestor's signature if they could write. This is a huge advantage. Those that do not have scanning equipment will send a typed or handwritten transcript that carries with it the possibility that an error might be made in transcription. If a copy of a signature

is important to you it might be a good idea to telephone in advance to check whether they do digital scanning or ask if it is possible for them to provide a photocopy of any signature.

It is important to remember that the primary function of a Register Office is what it always has been – to register current births, marriages and deaths. Some have enough staff to deal quickly and efficiently with family history requests. Other, smaller, offices may have to wait until they can fit it in with their day-to-day business but they will deal with your request in a friendly and sympathetic way and their local knowledge can be invaluable.

What does it cost?

The charge for a certificate direct from a Register Office is slightly less than from the GRO, and can be found on the website of any Register Office. Many will ask for a stamped addressed envelope. A short survey of a handful of offices found that the time taken to send the certificate varies from 'by return of post' to 'up to twenty-one days' depending on the policy of the individual office. Those that take longer might charge extra for a quicker service but in general the service from Register Offices is comparatively speedy.

There are some Register Offices, particularly in London, where the volume of work they have means that they simply cannot offer this service. This is particularly the case with marriages, where they might have to consult a lot of separate registers if they do not have a computerized index. In that case you have little option but to go to the GRO.

WHERE DO I GO FROM HERE?

Follow the advice given on the coloured pages opposite the copies of certificates of birth, marriage and death. Between 1841 and 1911 use the information you have found on your birth, marriage and death certificates to look at the ten-yearly census returns and pick up more family members (*see* Chapter 4). After 1911, the latest census currently available to us, go to newspapers to see if there was an announcement of the event (*see* Chapter 3). Check what you have found against family information if you have any. You can also use the addresses given to look at electoral registers and directories (*see* Chapter

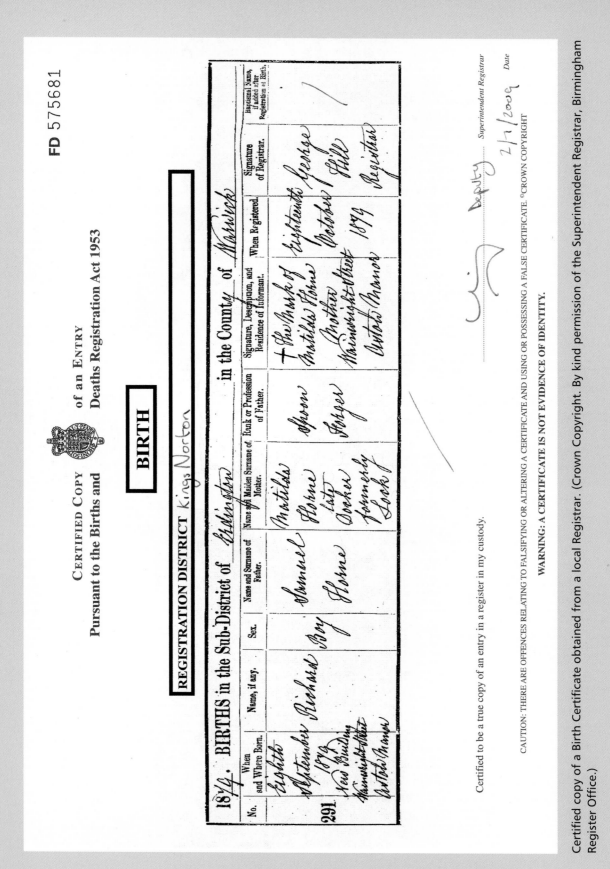

FD 575681

CERTIFIED COPY of an ENTRY
Pursuant to the Births and Deaths Registration Act 1953

BIRTH

REGISTRATION DISTRICT Kings Norton

1874. BIRTHS in the Sub-District of Edgbaston in the County of Warwick

No.	When and Where Born.	Name, if any.	Sex.	Name and Surname of Father.	Name and Maiden Surname of Mother.	Rank or Profession of Father.	Signature, Description, and Residence of Informant.	When Registered.	Signature of Registrar.	Baptismal Name, if added after Registration of Birth.
291	Eighth September Richard 1874 New Building Wainwright Street Aston Manor	Richard	Boy	Samuel Horne	Matilda Horne late Docker formerly Cook	Apron Forger	† The Mark of Matilda Horne Mother Wainwright Street Aston Manor	Eighteenth October 1874	George Hill Registrar	1

Certified to be a true copy of an entry in a register in my custody.

⎯⎯⎯⎯⎯ Deputy ⎯⎯⎯⎯⎯ Superintendent Registrar

2/7/2009 Date

Certified copy of a Birth Certificate obtained from a local Registrar. (Crown Copyright. By kind permission of the Superintendent Registrar, Birmingham Register Office.)

BIRTH CERTIFICATES

WHAT CAN A BIRTH CERTIFICATE TELL ME?

Pieces of the information provided on copy certificates of birth, marriage and death can be found elsewhere but, with one exception (see the section on Marriage Certificates), there is little likelihood of finding such detailed information anywhere else unless the original certificate is still in the family.

When you are making notes about your copy certificate, remember to note the name of the Registration District and Sub-district at the top of the certificate.

Up to 1 April 1969 the general layout of a birth certificate remained as shown in the example.

Number

Events were entered by the Registrars into their books in the order that people came in to report them. The General Register Office numbers were different because they are the result of a later copy. The GRO page number given for the birth of Richard Horne, for example, is 389 – totally different from the example shown which is a copy obtained from the local Registrar. This illustrates why, if you order a copy from the local Registrar, the GRO reference numbers will be of little help to them.

When and Where Born

The date of birth given is your starting point for other investigations into your ancestor. From 1875 there was a requirement to register a birth within six weeks so be a little bit wary of an exact six-week gap between the date of birth and the date of registration. The temptation was surely there to 'adjust' the date of birth a little to avoid late registration fees. (It can occasionally lead to the rather mystifying and inconvenient experience of finding a child baptized before his/her date of birth!) The parents of Richard Horne, in the example shown, were obviously cutting it a bit fine by registering over five weeks after the birth.

With the exception of some entries in the early days of registration, if a time of birth is given in this column it is likely that the birth was a multiple one so look in the General Register Office Index for other registrations with the same surname within the same Registration District. The address given here can be used to check against census returns (1841–1911), directories, electoral rolls and family information. This address is not necessarily going to be that of the family's home – the first-born child, in particular, was often born at the home of grandparents. Earlier certificates might just give the name of a village or town. If the birth took place in a hospital or institution it was quite common for the institution not to be named, but for an ordinary-looking address to be given; addresses of institutions are usually given in directories (see Chapter 3).

Name, if any

The name is the forename or names of the child as given by the person reporting the birth to the Registrar. You would hope to use this given name to follow the child through marriage and other records to an eventual death certificate. If you draw a blank on this it is possible that the registered name is not the name the child was known by later in life. Sometimes a birth was registered without a name in which case this column might be blank or have a line drawn through it. Unnamed children are described as 'Male' or 'Female' at the bottom of the relevant surname section in the General Register Office indexes.

Sex

This seems straightforward, but be aware that mistakes were occasionally made by midwives in identifying the sex of a child.

Name and Surname of Father

If the father's surname is a common one you need to be very sure that you have the right person by checking the address or occupation against that given in other certificates, census returns and trades directories. Bear in mind that occupations could change over the years and that descriptions of the same occupation might vary from region to region.

From 1875 if the birth was illegitimate this column is likely to be left blank or struck through unless the father was also present to register the birth. For this reason it has also been known for a family friend to 'stand in' as the father for the registration, to make it look better.

Name and Maiden Surname of Mother

If the mother had been married before then her previous married name might also be shown here. This information can be used to find the registered child's parents' marriage and the mother's previous marriage, if there is one shown. The more information you can accumulate the better, even if it does not seem immediately to be relevant to your search.

In the illustration, Lock was ('formerly') the maiden name of the mother and Docker ('late') was the name of her first husband. If the mother had been generally known by two names, possibly unconnected with marriage, her alias could be shown as 'otherwise….'. This column might also give you confirmation of a mother's unmarried status if no maiden name is shown.

Unmarried couples might answer the Registrar's questions as though they were married.

Rank or Profession of Father

The 'occupation' column can be very useful, particularly if the father's surname is a common one. Even so, occupations can vary over the years, particularly if a man's eyesight faded or he became physically unable to follow his trade, so the more examples you can find the more certain you will be that you have the right man. If the occupation is unfamiliar to you consult one of the many dictionaries of trades and occupations available (see Bibliography). You can also access online sources offering similar information. Websites tend to vary over time because many are on personal pages, but typing 'old trades and occupations' into a search engine should bring a result.

The word 'journeyman' can crop up quite frequently in connection with a trade. Journeymen were usually employed on a daily basis so had no guarantee of work from one day to the next, but the term is also used to denote someone who had learned a trade but not as an apprentice.

Signature, Description and Residence of Informant

If the informant, the person who talked to the Registrar to report the birth, was one of the parents then the information given is more likely to be accurate, particularly regarding the mother's maiden name and the father's occupation. If the informant was not one of the parents note the name and address because he or she could still turn out to be a relation. Over the years certain categories of people, including the mother and father, were allowed to register a birth. Apart from the parents, those present at the birth and managers of institutions were among the people most commonly found registering. Other categories were rather vague and could, in reality, cover just about anybody. After 1875 the father of an illegitimate child could only be named on the birth certificate if he was present with the mother to register the birth. Depending on where you get your copy of the certificate, you might also be lucky enough to have a useful copy of your ancestor's signature, if they were able to write.

When Registered

From 1875 the date of registration was obliged by law to be within six weeks of the birth. Note that Richard Horne, while born in September, was not registered until October and so appears in the December Quarter in the GRO indexes instead of the September Quarter as might be expected.

This is one of the few sources that can tell you with certainty that your ancestor was in a certain place on a certain day – particularly useful in connection with soldiers and sailors or other people who moved from place to place.

Baptismal Name if Added after Registration of Birth

A name could be added in this column up to twelve months after the registration of the birth. If no name was added within this time you might find the column has a line through it to avoid fraudulent additions later.

In the early years of registration people told the Registrar the information verbally rather than by filling in a form. Spelling would not necessarily come into the conversation and the Registrar would write down what he heard. If you are having difficulty finding your ancestor, try speaking the name with a local accent, or even a lisp. Remember that 'h' in particular might be dropped or added, 'j' and 'ch' can sound similar and 'r' can turn up in odd places. Try saying Richard Horne a few times, for example, and you could come up with Richard Orme or even Richard Dorne. Remember also that Horn and Horne would be listed separately in the indexes. Use your imagination – and be patient. Family history is full of stories of names not found for many years but eventually turning up in disguise. In any case do not expect spelling of a name to be consistent between certificates and census, for example. Too many different people had a hand in the process. By the twentieth century people were more educated and differences were fewer.

Do not expect your ancestors to be any more aware of the workings of officialdom than you are. If you cannot find a birth or death in the Registration District you expect, look at the neighbouring districts. Registration District boundaries were not known by the general public and they might have gone to the most convenient place to register the event or they might simply have moved a few streets away into the neighbouring district. Poorer people in towns and cities in particular would move house depending on their financial situation at the time, some staying just one step ahead of the rent man.

Civil registration dates to remember

1 July 1837: first certificates of birth, marriage and death issued in England and Wales. Deaths had to be registered within eight days.

1866: age of the deceased began to be included in the General Register Office indexes.

1875: registering a birth became compulsory under law. This had to be done within six weeks. There was a fine for failing to register or for late registration. The father of an illegitimate child had to be present at the registration if he wanted his name on the certificate. The time allowed for registering a death was reduced to five days.

1898: a registrar no longer needed to be present at all non-conformist or Catholic marriages.

1911: mother's maiden name now included in GRO birth index.

1911: surname of the spouse now included in GRO marriage index.

1927: a formal register for adoptions began. Before this date adoption was largely informal and it is very difficult to find written proof except in family papers or wills. Parents could re-register illegitimate births if they married.

1929: legal age for marriage changed from fourteen (for boys) and twelve (for girls) to sixteen for both sexes. Permission of parents needed up to twenty-one.

1969: format of birth and death certificates changed. Date of birth now shown in GRO death indexes. Age of majority reduced to eighteen. Parents could re-register illegitimate births to include father's name even if they had not married.

---

3) to try to establish how long people were at the addresses given.

One obvious link to make from a death certificate is to go in search of a will (*see* Chapter 5). Not everyone made a will, but a surprising number did, and they were not all well off. Also try to find where the person was buried because there might be a burial entry or a monumental inscription to give more information (*see* Chapter 6 and Chapter 11).

If it is obvious from any of the certificates that there was one, try to find the previous marriage. If the father of the bride or groom is described as 'deceased' on the marriage certificate, do a search for his death certificate or burial. Not everyone told the truth about this, or even knew whether their father was alive or dead.

Note, from the ages of the people involved, whether they were of an age to serve in the armed forces during either of the World Wars and pursue that line of enquiry with the help of the information in Chapter 9. Check to see whether there are any sources you might follow up in relation to people's occupations, given on the certificates (*see* Chapter 11). Keep looking at your certificates again and again through your research to see if new discoveries you have made in the meantime give some additional meaning to the information they contain.

CERTIFIED COPY OF AN ENTRY OF DEATH

REGISTRATION DISTRICT _____ Walsall

DEATH in the Sub-district of ___ Walsall _____ in the _____ County of Stafford

No.	When and where died	Name and surname	Sex	Age	Occupation	Cause of death	Signature, description and residence of informant	When registered	Signature of registrar
Columns:-	1	2	3	4	5	6	7	8	9
188	Sixth July 1868 at Patsey in the Parish of Walsall	Edward Stranger	Male	28 years	A Plate by trade	Accidentally drowned while Bathing in a Pit at Patsey	Information received from A.A.Fletcher Coroner for Walsall Inquest held 13th July, 1868	Seventeenth July 24th 1868	J.W.Detty Registrar

CERTIFIED to be a true copy of an entry in the certified copy of a Register of Deaths in the District above mentioned.

Given at the GENERAL REGISTER OFFICE, under the Seal of the said Office, the .... 24th .... day of ...February... 2000

DXZ 686180

DEATH CERTIFICATES

WHAT CAN I LEARN FROM A DEATH CERTIFICATE?

Some family historians regard death certificates as unimportant, but they can be a mine of useful information, leading to other important sources. Also, there is a high chance of finding a death certificate because a person's birth might not have been registered, he or she may not have married but everyone dies sooner or later. It is often said by those with the most experience that you can't prove a life unless you can prove the death, added to which, from 1837, a death certificate had to be produced in order for someone to be buried.

Don't forget to note the Registration District details from the top of the certificate. They will be useful if you are looking for other information for the same family.

Number

Events were entered by the Registrars into their books in the order that people came in to report them. The General Register Office numbers were different because they are the result of a later copy.

When and Where Died

You can use the address given in this column to check against census returns and other documents to assist in identification of your ancestor. In the example shown, the death was accidental and the home address is not given. Note that, in any case, the place of death is not necessarily the usual address of the person who died. If it is not a hospital or workhouse it is possible that the address was at least the home of a relative.

Once you have the date of death you can go to church and cemetery records to look for a burial and to newspapers for an obituary. Prisons and hospitals were sometimes identified by an ordinary looking address, and not the name of the institution.

Name and Surname

Variations in name and spelling might occur if the person reporting the death was not a close relative. Also, the name a person had when they died is not always the name on their birth certificate – married women are the most

obvious example. At its most simple someone might have been given two Christian names at birth and used the second rather than the first. An illegitimate child would usually have been given his mother's surname on the birth certificate but might have used that of his father or step-father while growing up. Or, the most difficult to trace, someone who just changed his name to one totally unrelated to the one he was born with.

Sex

With some reported deaths the sex might be all that is known of a person. People did not generally carry documentary proof of who they were and, if a body was found by the roadside, the person might remain unidentified.

Age

Take note of who is reporting the death. Even children of the deceased might be a little vague as to their exact age and if the person reporting is a neighbour or the master of a workhouse then the information could be some way out. A spouse is the most likely person to know the exact age but if a person has 'adjusted' their age at some point in their life – for example stating they were twenty-one in order to marry under age or adjusting it upwards to join the army – they might have stuck to that age for the rest of their life leaving even close relatives in the dark.

Rank or Profession

With a male death the rank or profession given should bear some relation to information given in census returns and other documents. A married female's death certificate will usually say whose wife or widow she was, and give her husband's occupation. If she was a widow this will give you a clear date from which to work in looking for the death and burial of the husband. A child's death certificate might say 'son of' or 'daughter of' and give the father's name. In the example given Edward Stringer's occupation is given as 'A Plater by trade'. The words 'by trade' might imply that he did not work at his trade very often.

Cause of Death

The cause of death given in the example is fairly straightforward – an accidental drowning 'while Bathing in a Pool

at Palfrey'. Some causes of death are less understandable to a lay person but there are medical dictionaries and websites to demystify the terminology. Website addresses change because many are personal ones but typing 'archaic medical terms' into a search engine should bring a result. Page 42 shows a newspaper report about the inquest into this particular death.)

Doctors did not attend everyone who was ill or dying. Before the introduction of the National Health Service doctors had to be paid and many ordinary people could not afford their services. If an entry gives a cause of death as 'certified', it means that a doctor signed a death certificate. From 1875 a doctor's certificate was required before a death certificate could be issued, and the doctor's name and qualification were shown.

Signature, Description and Residence of Informant

The informant in this case is the local coroner. If the cause of death was an accident this column should indicate whether an inquest was held. Inquests were often reported in newspapers even if the original coroner's report has not survived, or is within the 75-year closure period for coroner's reports, so the date given in the example could lead you to further detail about the death.

If an informant is described as 'Present at the Death' they were there when the person died. If they are described as 'In Attendance' it means that they attended the Register Office to report the death.

The person reporting a death was often a relative, so note the name and address and see if you can find out more about them even if the surname does not match that of the deceased. This is often the way you can find out the married name of a daughter, and then follow it up by looking for a marriage. After 1875 the relationship of the 'informant' to the deceased had to be given.

When Registered

From 1837 a death had to be registered within eight days and from 1875 this was reduced to five days. However, if there was a post-mortem or inquest the time between death and registration might be extended. This might affect the quarter in which the death would be shown in the GRO Indexes.

1876. Marriage solemnized at *Christ Church* in the *Parish of West Bromwich* in the County of *Stafford*

No.	When Married.	Name and Surname.	Age.	Condition.	Rank or Profession.	Residence at the time of Marriage.	Father's Name and Surname.	Rank or Profession of Father.
97	Dec 25th 1876	Edwin Jones	23	Bachelor	Iron worker	Bradbury Manchester	Thomas Jones	Groom
		Mary Ann Beatley	22	Spinster	—	West Bromwich	Job Beatley	Lasgones

Married in the *Christ Parish Church* according to the Rites and Ceremonies of the Established Church, by

This Marriage was solemnized between us, { Edwin Jones
Mary Ann Beatley }

in the Presence of us, { Henry Jones
Elizabeth Smith }

A certified copy of a Marriage Certificate from the General Register Office. (Crown Copyright.)

MARRIAGE CERTIFICATES

WHAT CAN I LEARN FROM A MARRIAGE CERTIFICATE?

When noting the date and place of a marriage do not forget to note the name of the church, if it was a church wedding, and the county in which the marriage took place in addition to the name of the Registration District. The church and county information will be helpful in going backwards from 1837. The Registration District information might help you to find other events registered for the same family from 1837 onwards.

Number

The numbers in the GRO Indexes generally only mean something to the GRO, but can be helpful in finding the correct certificate.

When Married

In a neat and ordered world one might start looking for the birth or baptism of the first child nine months after the marriage. However, it was not unusual, particularly in earlier years, for the date of marriage to be after the date of birth of the first child. It was also not uncommon for the bride to be pregnant at the time of the marriage.

Name and Surname

This information is only as accurate as the bride and groom wished it to be. If a woman was a widow her previous married name will usually be given here.

Age

This is an interesting one. You would be advised to treat with suspicion anyone giving their age as exactly twenty-one because they might have lied to avoid having to gain parental approval for the marriage – or not really been sure how old they were anyway. Women marrying younger men, and also men marrying younger women might knock a year or two off their real age. 'Of full age' means twenty-one or over. A 'minor' would be under twenty-one (until 1969, when the age of majority changed from twenty-one to eighteen). Up to 1929 the legal age at which a girl could marry with parental consent was twelve and a boy fourteen. Marriages at that age were a fairly rare occurrence, however.

Ages given on many marriage certificates might often be regarded as a useful starting point for research rather than the gospel truth. Even so, they are useful points of comparison with census returns and other certificates particularly if, having lied about their age in order to marry, a person continued to do so consistently through the rest of their life.

Condition

Bachelor, spinster, widow or widower – again, we are relying on people to tell the truth. If you have a widow or widower you have potentially twice as much information available to you and a point of reference for checking the accuracy of the certificate you already hold. Look for the first marriage and the death of the previous spouse.

In later years divorcees might be shown as such but sometimes appear as bachelors or spinsters, nevertheless.

Rank or Profession

The groom's occupation is another useful identification point to compare with other sources of information. Even if the woman did work it was rarely shown on the marriage certificate until at least the mid-twentieth century, even if she had a responsible professional job, because the man was, in theory at least, supposed to be able to support her. She might not even have been asked what she did. Edwin Jones, in the example shown, continued to work with iron (see page 57).

Bear in mind that, on a big occasion, the groom might have inflated his status slightly, for example, Farmer instead of Agricultural Labourer.

Residence at the Time of Marriage

If the marriage was in church, at least one of the parties should have been resident in the parish for a number of weeks prior to the event. The same address for both parties commonly appears but might be the address of a relative they were staying with for the sake of convenience. Sometimes just the name of a village might appear but later addresses tend to be more specific.

If the residence of one of the parties was outside the parish where the marriage was taking place, as in the example shown, you have a second chance of finding a banns register.

Father's Name and Surname

This is one of the chief reasons that marriage certificates are worth the effort of searching. The father's name can take you back to another generation and confirm information on a birth certificate. If a woman was a widow the father's surname will usually be her maiden name. If no father's name appears it is possible that the person was illegitimate and if no father's name was given at the time of the marriage there is likely to be a line through this column.

If the father was dead at the time of the marriage the word 'deceased' should appear in brackets. There is no guarantee that this was the case so check census information to confirm it and look for his death certificate as proof. Equally, if a father is not described as 'deceased' it does not mean he was still alive – so seek corroboration. An illegitimate bride or groom might describe a fictitious or long-gone father as 'deceased' to save embarrassment.

Rank or Profession of Father

This was based on information given at the time of the marriage, so might be designed to impress. If the father was now sick or in the workhouse but had once been a Master Carpenter then the latter is most likely to be cited.

Was the Marriage by Banns or by Licence?

Banns were generally called or published for three weeks prior to the marriage in the parishes of both parties, although some marriages did not take place immediately after the third time. Banns currently remain valid for three months. Some separate banns registers survive in parish records and might contain additional information (see Chapter 6).

If the marriage was by licence there is a chance that the licence has survived and can be found in a county and/or diocesan archive. A marriage licence can give additional family information and is definitely worth looking for (see Chapter 6).

Signatures of both Parties to the Marriage

The original signatures of both parties should be on the original Parish Register, if they could write, and possibly on a digital copy of the marriage certificate obtained from the local Registrar if they have the facilities to reproduce them. The original signatures or marks will not be on a certificate obtained from the GRO, as in the example, because these are the quarterly copies done at a later date.

Signatures of Witnesses

Witnesses were often family members so it is wise to take careful note of their names.

A page from *Bisset's Magnificent Guide or Grand Copperplate Directory for the Town of Birmingham 1808*. Plate 18. (Reproduced with the permission of Birmingham Libraries and Archives.)

3 Trades Directories, Newspapers and Electoral Registers

TRADES DIRECTORIES

Why do I need them?

Trades directories are among very few original sources you can go to where people might, at the time, have been listed alphabetically. They were at their peak during Victorian times. The bare minimum of what you can get from a directory is the fact that someone of the same or similar name and occupation to your ancestor lived at a certain address. It will not give you specific information about family connections. However, when used with other documents, a 'find' in a directory can be worth a great deal.

Most directories are simply printed lists of people in a trade or profession in a particular town or county, sometimes with householders listed and maps attached. However, there was fierce competition between publishers in some areas. This produced a few interesting variations, like the example opposite from *Bisset's Magnificent Guide or Grand Copperplate Directory for the Town of Birmingham 1808* – described by the author in his introduction as a 'nominal Concatenation, alphabetically arranged, and engraved in such a superb manner...' that it would do away with the need for business cards altogether! Many directories also included town and county maps which can give you a good idea of how people might have travelled from one place to another at the time – useful if your ancestor moved.

What dates do they cover?

The largest number of trades' directories – chiefly Pigot's, Kelly's, White's and Post Office Directories – cover much of the nineteenth century and the early part of the twentieth century. Other, smaller, publishers came and went. The earliest directories now available were mostly printed in the mid- to late-eighteenth century as demand arose for accurate information about opportunities for doing business in the growing towns and cities. These early directories are rarer and generally include fewer names – but it is always worth the time spent looking.

The number of trades directories became fewer after the Second World War but there are still some published today.

What can they tell me?

From 1841 to 1911 (the first and latest available national census records) trades directories can provide a useful back-up to census returns (*see* Chapter 4), filling out the ten years between each census by, if you are lucky, telling you whether your ancestor remained at the address given in the census. Up to 1841 and after 1911 they assume an even greater importance because they can help to guide you towards other sources such as parish registers, electoral registers and certificates of birth marriage and death.

If you consult not just one directory but several, over the adult lifetime of your ancestor, you might be able to trace his or her movements and gain clues as to their date of death. For example, if an entry for Thomas Smith at a particular address in one year is replaced by Mrs Smith at the same address the following year you might start

Worcestershire.   KIDDERMINSTER, &c.   Pigot & Co.'s

COACHES—Continued.

To LUDLOW, the *Union* (from Birmingham) every day at twelve; goes through Bewdley and Cleobury Mortimer.

To SHREWSBURY, the *Hawk* (from Cheltenham) every afternoon (Sunday excepted) at half-past two; goes through Bridgnorth.

To STOURPORT, the *Royal Mail* (from Birmingham) every morning at half-past ten; goes through Bewdley.

To WOLVERHAMPTON, the *Bang-Up* (from Worcester) every morning (Sunday excepted) at nine, and the *Everlasting*, every afternoon (Sunday excepted) at half-past five; both go through Stourbridge and Dudley.

To WORCESTER, the *Everlasting* (from Wolverhampton) every morning (Sunday excepted) at half-past eight, and the *Bang-Up*, every evening (Sun. exceptd) at half-past six; both go through Stourport and Ombersley.

CARRIERS.

To LONDON, Bloomfield and Co. from the Swan, three times a week—Haines, Bland and Co. from the Black Star, every Tuesday, Thursday & Saturday—and John Jolly, from his warehouse, every Monday, Thursday & Saturday.

To BIRMINGHAM, John Bennett, from the Black Bull, every Monday & Thursday—John Farmer, from the Black Bull, and Thomas Fawkner, from the Bell, every Tuesday and Friday—and Saml. Dodd, from the Black Bull, every Fridy.

To BRIDGNORTH, George Broad, from the Bell, every Mon. Wednes. & Satur.

To BRISTOL, Haines, Bland and Co. from the Black Star, every Tuesday, Thursday and Saturday.

To KNIGHTON, Samuel Dodd, calls at the Black Bull, every Monday.

To LUDLOW, John Farmer, from the Black Bull, every Monday & Thursday.

To STOURBRIDGE, James Gardener, from the Three Tuns, every day (Sun.ex.)

To WOLVERHAMPTON, John Jolly, from his warehouse, every Monday.

To WORCESTER, Samuel Cole, from the Bell, every Monday, Wednesday and Saturday—and James Gardener, from the Three Tuns, every day (Friday and Sunday excepted.)

CONVEYANCE BY WATER.

To LONDON & all intermediate places, Pickford and Co. from Park wharf, every Tuesday, Thursday & Saturday—and Crowley, Hicklin, Batty and Co. from Old wharf, every Monday, Thursday and Saturday.

To MANCHESTER and LIVERPOOL, Matthew Heath, Shiptons and Co. and Worthington & Co. from the Old wharf, three times a week.

To SHARDLOW & STOURBRIDGE, Ames and Co. & Matthew Heath, from the Old wharf, three times a week—and Barnett and Worthington, once a week.

GREAT MALVERN

IS a delightful village and fashionable watering place, in the parish of its name, in the lower division of the hundred of Pershore, 120 miles w.by N. from London, 8 w. from Worcester, 24 E. by N. from the city of Hereford, and 45 E. from Hay, in South Wales; romantically situate on the eastern declivity of a range of hills separating the counties of Worcester and Hereford, and extending from north to south for nearly nine miles, the greatest height being one thousand four hundred and forty feet, and varying from one to two miles in breadth from east to west: of these the most prominent are, the Worcestershire and Herefordshire beacons, the summits of which command most extensive and interesting views of the surrounding country; comprehending in the distance, the counties of Radnor, Brecon, Salop, Warwick, and Stafford; and nearer the counties of Worcester, Hereford, and Gloucester, with their stately cathedrals, together with the fertile and richly cultivated tract of country, watered by the Severn, and finely clothed with wood. These hills possess the advantage of a most salubrious air, but their principal celebrity arises from the wells, which are chalybeate and bituminous, the water of which, is remarkable for its purity, and for its gentle aperient and diuretic properties: the former is in the eastern part of the village near the church; the latter called 'Holywell', is situate two miles to the south of it. On the eastern ridge of the Hill and at St. Ann's Well, on the north side of the Worcestershire beacon, there are some respectable hotels, and every accommodation has been provided for drinking the waters, and for hot and cold bathing. The more ancient portion of the village is irregularly built, and consists of houses scattered on the declivity of the mountain; but since the celebrity of the springs and the purity of the air, have made it a place of fashionable resort, handsome ranges of modern houses have been erected. The public library is a neat building of the Doric order. The hotels and lodging-houses afford every comfort that the invalid or visiter on pleasure can require; and in every direction there are romantic and agreeable walks.

The parish church, dedicated to St. Mary, is a venerable and elegant cruciform structure, combining the Norman, and the later styles of English architecture, with a fine square embattled tower, rising from the centre. The chancel is lighted by a fine range of windows, with rich and elegant tracery; the east window, and that in the north transept, are particularly beautiful, and several portions of the ancient stained glass, carved seats, and other evidences of its antiquity are remaining. Some few years since the church was repaired and beautified, and it has subsequently received an addition of three hundred and eighty sittings. The living is a discharged vicarage, in the patronage of Thomas Edward Foley, Esq. who is lord of the manor. There is a place of worship for methodists; a Sunday school, in which about one hundred children are instructed, and a school of industry. The parish of Great Malvern (including the chapelry of NEWLAND), contained, according to the government census taken in 1831, 2,140 inhabitants, being an increase in the population, in thirty years, of 1,189 persons.

POST OFFICE, John Mason, *Post Master.*—Letters from LONDON, BIRMINGHAM, WORCESTER, &c. arrive every forenoon at eleven, and are despatched every afternoon at three.—Letters from SOUTH WALES, HEREFORD, &c. arrive every evening at twenty minutes before seven, and are despatched every morning at half-past seven.

NOBILITY, GENTRY AND CLERGY.

Baker Mrs. —, Malvern
Beauchamp Right Hon. the Earl of, Maddersfield and Court
Benson G. M. esq. Wells
Berrington William, esq. Wells
Campbell Miss Jane, Malvern
Candler Miss Isabella, Malvern
Candler Captain William, Malvern
Card Rev. Henry, D. D. Malvern
Carter Major Henry, Link
Cook Rev. George, Malvern
Dandridge Miss —, Malvern
Day Captain —, Malvern
Dent —, esq. Malvern
Essington Wm. W. esq. Malvern
Garlike Wm. Bennett, esq. Malvern
Haddington the Countess of, Malvrn
Hill Thomas, esq. Malvern
Hornyold Ths. esq. Blackmore park
Lechmere Sir Anthony, Rhydd
Lechmere Edwd. H. esq. Malvern
Longworth William, esq. Malvern
Lyttelton Right Hon. Lady Aphia
Mason Oliver, esq. Malvern

Morsby the Misses —, Malvern
Moseley the Misses Harriet and Fanny, Malvern
Plumptree the Misses, Malvern
Steers Miss Fanny, Priory
Walker Mrs. —, Peckham grove
Wilmot Lady Mary Ann, Malvern
Witts Captain —, Malvern
Wood Rev. J., Malvern
Woodyatt Thomas, esq. Malvern

PROFESSIONAL PERSONS.

Addison William, surgeon
Ballard Philip, attorney
Elgie Matthew and Thomas (solicitors to Great Malvern association for the prosecution of felons) 48 Broad street, Worcester
Salmons the Misses, ladies' boarding academy   [classics
Simons Edward, teacher of the West and Son, surgeons

INNS, HOTELS, AND POSTING HOUSES.

Admiral Benbow, Ths. Cook, Wells
Belle View, Charles Clarke
Crown, Andrew Morrison

Essington's, Hanh. Essington, Wells
Foley Arms, John Archer
Well House, John Nichols, Wells

PUBLIC HOUSES.

Fermor Arms, William Harrison
Lion, Henry Lane
Unicorn, Samuel Roe (& maltster and butcher)

SHOPKEEPERS & TRADERS.

Adams Thomas, plumber, &c.
Allen Wm. gardener & seedsman
Archer Thomas, joiner, &c.
Bellers Elizabeth, maltster
Berry Thomas, shoe maker
Broad James, plumber
Burston John, blacksmith
Clay Frederick, tailor
Clifton John, bricklayer
Collins Thomas, hair dresser
Dalby Richard, corn miller
Davis Henry, plumber
Dawes Henry, coal merchant
Doidge George, plumber
Dryden George, chymist, &c.
Evans Edward, confectioner
George Thomas, blacksmith

648

Directory. GREAT MALVERN. **Worcestershire.**

Griffiths William, grocer & draper
Grimley Edward, tailor
Harrington Thomas, plumber
Hayes Richard, plasterer
Hudson Ann, dress maker
Lamb Henry, stationer, and circulating library
Lane John, saddler
Lucas Thomas, shopkeeper
Lumney Thomas, stone mason
M'Camm George, plasterer
M'Camm Thomas, bricklayer
Maggs and Co. drapers
Morgan William, joiner
Morison William, brewer & coal merchant
Phillpots John, shopkeeper
Phillpots Richard, joiner
Preece Thomas, boot & shoe maker
Roberts Isaac, miller
Southall John, stationer
Stokes Thomas, grocer

Towndrow William, grocer
Trinder William, confectioner
Walker James, butcher
Warwick and Fernyhough, drapers
Wells James, straw hat maker
Whiteing William, gardener and seedsman [billiard rooms
Williams Thos. keeper of baths and

COACHES,

PASSING THROUGH MALVERN.

To LONDON, the *Sovereign*, every morning at six; goes through Worcester, Pershore, Evesham, Broadway, Moreton, Chipping Norton, Woodstock, Oxford, &c.
To BRECON, the *Telegraph* (from Worcester) every Tuesday, Thursday and Saturday at twelve noon; goes thro' Ledbury, Hereford, Hay, Brecon, &c.
To CARMARTHEN, the *Cambrian* (from Worcester) every Monday, Wednesday and Friday morning at seven; goes through Ledbury, Hereford, Hay, &c.

To CHELTENHAM, the *Gazelle* (from Worcester) every afternoon at four, and the *Tally-Ho*, every afternoon at three; both go through Upton & Tewkesbury.
To HEREFORD, the *Telegraph* (from Worcester) every Monday, Wednesday and Friday at twelve noon.
To LEDBURY, the *Magnet* (from Worcester) every evening at six.
To WORCESTER, the *Magnet* (from Ledbury) every morning at ten—the *Gazelle* (from Cheltenham) every day at twelve—the *Telegraph* (from Brecon) every Monday, Wednesday and Friday afternoon at half-past one—the *Telegraph* (from Hereford) every Tuesday, Thursday and Saturday afternoon at half-past one—and the *Cambrian* (from Carmarthen) every Tuesday, Thursday and Saturday night at nine.

CARRIERS.

To WORCESTER, William Baylis, Robert Burston, Thomas Walker, Wm. Gage, William Matthews and Timothy Tippings, every Mon. Wed. and Satur.

PERSHORE AND NEIGHBOURHOOD.

PERSHORE is a market town, partly in the parish of St. Andrew, and partly in that of Holy Cross, in the upper division of the hundred of its name; 102 miles N. W. by W. from London, 9 S. E. from Worcester, and 10 N. by E. from Tewkesbury; situate on the lower road from Worcester to London, and on the western bank of the river Avon, which is here navigable, and is crossed by a bridge on the south. The name of this place has been variously spelt *Persore, Pearshore*, and, lastly, that which it now retains, 'Pershore:' the appellation is supposed, by Camden, to be derived from *Periscoran*, in allusion to the numerous pear-trees which at one time grew in its vicinity. The town, which consists chiefly of one street, well paved, and of considerable length, is remarkable for its neatness; and the vicinity of it is very delightful, presenting many pleasing prospects over a country naturally fertile, and which is rendered still more beautiful by the labours of the husbandman; being also ornamented by several seats belonging to distinguished individuals, among which are 'Crome House,' the residence of the Right Hon. the Earl of Coventry; 'Elmley Park,' the seat of Col. T. H. H. Davies, &c. The trade of Pershore has suffered a great diminution of late years: the principal branches now existing are woolstapling and malting, the former being the most considerable: main springs for watches were at one time manufactured here extensively, but at present there is but one person thus employed. The retail trade of the place is somewhat advantaged by the respectability of the neighbourhood, together with its thoroughfare situation; and for the accommodation of travellers there are some good inns, one of which, the 'Angel,' is a respectable posting-house. The dean and chapter of Worcester are lords

of the manor of Benholme, and Sir John Sebright, Bart. possesses the manorial rights of Pershore Old-lands and Pershore New-lands : a court-leet is held for each manor annually, at one of which a constable is appointed. This town returned two burgesses to parliament in the reign of Edward I, since which period the privilege has been discontinued. Under the new *Boundary Act* (an appendage to the Reform Bill,) Pershore is appointed one of the polling stations at the election of members to represent, in parliament, the eastern division of the county.

The places of worship are, two churches, belonging to the parishes before-mentioned, and a chapel for the baptists. St. Andrew's consists of a choir and south transept, the remains of a noble cruciform church : the living is a discharged vicarage, in the patronage of the dean and chapter of Worcester, and incumbency of the Rev. John Palmer. The church of the Holy Cross was formerly conventual, having belonged to the abbey, existing here at the time of the dissolution, but of which there are no remains, except the church and the abbey-house : the living is held, as a curacy, with the vicarage of St. Andrew's, in the same presentation as that living : the Rev. John Foley is the present minister. Pershore is said to have been the birth-place of Samuel Butler, author of 'Hudibras,' a celebrated satirical poem. The market, which is held on Tuesday, is very thinly attended : the fairs take place on the Tuesday in Easter-week, the 26th of June, and the last Tuesday in October, chiefly for horses. The whole of the two parishes of St. Andrew and Holy Cross contained, in 1821, 3,892 inhabitants, and in 1831, 4,225; of which last number those parts of the parishes forming the town contained 2,536 persons.

POST OFFICE, High-street, William Giles, *Post Master*.—Letters from LONDON arrive every morning at eight, and are despatched every evening at half-past five.

NOBILITY, GENTRY AND CLERGY.

Amherst Mrs. —, Pershore
Amherst Jeffrey, R. N. Pershore
Bedford John, esq. Abbey house
Burne John, esq. High st
Coventry the Right Hon. Earl of, Croome house
Davies Rev. B. Pershore
Davies Colonel T. H. H. Elmley park
Dineley Rev. George, High st
Fenwick Nicholas Lewis, esq. Besford Court
Foley Rev. John, Pershore
Hanford Charles, esq. Woollashill
Hudson George B. esq. Myrtle
Hudson Henry, esq. Wick
Hudson Richard, esq. Wick house
Hunter John, esq. High st
Keene Rev. Thomas C. Pershore
Landor R.E. esq. Birlingham rectory
Marriott Major-General, Avon bank
Palmer Rev. John, Pershore
Parker Rev. Hubert, Gt. Cumberton

Parker Rev. John, Little Cumberton
Porter Mr. Thomas C. Birlingham
Whitaker Mrs. —, Pershore
Woodward Herbert, esq. High st

ACADEMIES & SCHOOLS.

Bushell J. E. (gentlemen's)
Reynolds Miss E. (ladies' boarding)
Roberts Frances (ladies' boarding)
Roberts William (gentlemen's)

ATTORNEYS.

Oldaker Edmund & Charles
Woodward & Wheatley
Woodward Francis

BAKERS & FLOUR DEALERS.

Andrews Edmund
Edwards John
Handy John
Henley William
Howse John
Melin Charles

BASKET MAKERS.

Badger Joseph
Farley John
Turvey Henry

BLACKSMITHS.

Checketts William
Gwilliam James
Taylor William

BOOT AND SHOE MAKERS.

Farley Joseph
Hooper Edward
Miles William
Phillips William
Salsbury William
Tyler Robert
Wheeler Richard

BUTCHERS.

Broomfield William
Evans Honey
Forster William
Meredith Edward
Stephens John
Workman Sarah

CARPENTERS & JOINERS.

Clarke Samuel
Hope Richard
Stephens Richard

82

Census dates

1841 Sunday 6 June
1851 Sunday 30 March
1861 Sunday 7 April
1871 Sunday 2 April
1881 Sunday 3 April
1891 Sunday 5 April
1901 Sunday 31 March
1911 Sunday 2 April

Since 1841, when the census was held in early June, the census has been held consistently in late March and early April. It has been suggested that, because many agricultural workers were away from home during the summer months, the 1841 census enumerators might not have been able to find them if they were on the road looking for work. From 1851 onwards the date was changed.

the years, and still does – to identify anyone not at home, or without a permanent home and try to obtain their details. Some were more conscientious than others.

Where can I see it?
The 1911 census is available online at the Findmypast website. You can see it free of charge at the National Archives at Kew, London, with payment only for paper copies of the images. Other places where free access to the 1911 census has been arranged are:

- Birmingham Archives and Heritage
- Devon Record Office (Exeter)
- The National Library of Wales, Aberystwyth
- Manchester Archives and Local Studies and Gtr. Manchester County Record Office
- Norfolk Record Office
- Nottinghamshire Archives
- Tyne and Wear Archives

Where can I see other census returns?
Research in census returns has been transformed in the twenty-first century by the digitization and indexing projects undertaken by various commercial enterprises in co-operation with the National Archives, who hold the originals. We are now spoiled for choice because there are several websites we can pay to go to and type in a name in the hope of finding our ancestors in one of the censuses from 1841 to 1901. There is a list of the main providers in Chapter 1. Some have indexed the whole range of census years and some have fewer available although eventually they are likely to compete on more equal terms. Chapter 1 discusses ways of choosing and using online providers. There you will also find other ways of accessing census information online, some of them free.

Censuses 1841 to 1891 have been available for years on microfilm at local and county archives and appear likely still to be available in this form for some time to come. The 1901 and 1911 census were the first to be made available online and it is through online providers that you are most likely to have to get to them. This does not mean that you will have to pay to do so because some large libraries and archives have access to one of the main providers free, or for a minimal fee for use of the computer.

WHERE DO I GO FROM HERE?
See the section opposite the 1871 example for some suggestions. Also, be constantly aware that people did not always tell the truth to government officials so it would be wise to test everything they have said to a census enumerator against other information.

The census is one of your best chances of finding a lot of personal information about your ancestors in one set of documents. Be sure to use it well by following up everything you find and looking at every census year available for the family you are looking for, and to build up a picture of the wider family. This will help to place 'your' family in context and help you to identify them going further back in time. The years before 1841, when the earliest national census returns are available to you, are generally more difficult to research so you need to establish a solid foundation from which to move backwards.

CENSUS OF ENGLAND AND WALES, 1911.

Before writing on this Schedule please read the Examples and the Instructions given on the other side of the paper, as well as the headings of the Columns. The entries should be written in Ink.

The contents of the Schedule will be treated as confidential. Strict care will be taken that no information is disclosed with regard to individual persons. The returns are not to be used for proof of age, as in connection with Old Age Pensions, or for any other purpose than the preparation of Statistical Tables.

NAME AND SURNAME	RELATIONSHIP to Head of Family.	AGE (last Birthday) and SEX		PARTICULARS as to MARRIAGE					PROFESSION or OCCUPATION of Persons aged ten years and upwards.			BIRTHPLACE of every person.	NATIONALITY of every Person born in a Foreign Country.	INFIRMITY.
		Ages of Males.	Ages of Females.	Write "Single," "Married," "Widower," or "Widow"	Completed years the present Marriage has lasted.	Total Children Born Alive.	Children still Living.	Children who have Died.	Personal Occupation.	Industry or Service with which worker is connected.	Whether Employer, Worker, or Own Account.	Whether Working at Home.			
Edwin Jones	Head	55		Married	33	6	6	0	Hoar Shoe Rotter (?)	Iron Tin Manufactory			Staffordshire Shelton	British	
Mary Ann Jones	Wife		54	Married	33	6	6	0					Northwich	British	
Harry Jones	Son	25		Single					Draper	Draper	26		Rhos, Isle N.S.W.	British	
Mary Edith Jones	daughter		23	Single					Science	Science	270	Teacher	Rhos School N.S.W.	British	
Ethel Jane Jones	Daughter		18	Single					Laundry sorting	stitches	704	Worker	Lancashire Wigan	1864	
Fred Jones	Son	21		Single					Machinist	Machinist	270	Worker	Lancashire Penditton	06.8	
Lillian Jones	Daughter		16	Single					Tailoress	Clothing factory		Worker	" Wigan	06.8	

(To be filled up by the Enumerator.)

	Males.	Females.	Total Persons.
	3	4	7

Initials of Enumerator. *(illegible)*

(To be filled up by, or on behalf of, the Head of Family or other person in occupation, or in charge, of this dwelling.)

Write below the Number of Rooms in this Dwelling (House, Tenement, or Apartment). Count the kitchen as a room but do not count scullery, landing, lobby, closet, bathroom; nor warehouse, office, shop.

6

I declare that this Schedule is correctly filled up to the best of my knowledge and belief.

Signature *Edwin Jones*

Postal Address *45 Hillary Street, Flash, Walsall*

1911 census Walsall, Staffordshire. (Crown Copyright. Courtesy The National Archives ref. RG14PN17185 RG78PN1057 RD370 SD3 ED28 SN76.)

Getting the best out of name indexes

When you use an electronic index to look for a name in a census return you have to consider that at least two groups of people might have made mistakes that will make your search difficult. One is the combination of the original enumerator and the family who filled in the schedule. They might have made a mistake in the return itself, or even missed making the entry altogether. The other grouping consists of the people who, much more recently, have tried to read the return, transcribe it and make up the electronic index you are looking at. Hardly surprising, then, that some names are difficult to find.

There are several things you can do to try to find someone who is proving elusive. Try a different name index from a different online provider. Free indexes are available at the FreeCEN website, although coverage is not complete. Also, the Familysearch website has a free index of the 1881 census.

Sme Family History Societies have produced their own name indexes. These have the advantage of having been done by family historians and might therefore be expected to have a high level of accuracy. Some are available on CD from the societies themselves or via the GENfair website. The 1851 census, in particular, was widely indexed by Family History Societies in book form before the advent of online indexes. These books are often still available on library shelves and at the library of the Society of Genealogists.

When dealing with electronic name indexes, look carefully at the instructions provided. (They do seem to differ between different indexes.) How, for example, do they deal with abbreviations? Would a search for William Wilson in the 1871 example also bring up Wm. Wilson? Or is it necessary to do a separate search? What provision have they made for surname searches using substitutions such as * for missing letters? Be sure you understand the system

you are using. Using William as an example, again, was he simply known as Bill? And would that come up under a search for William?

Try looking for a brother or sister with a slightly less common name. A search for a William or a Thomas with a common surname, like young William Wilson in 1871 – and with no address to go by – might give you far too many results to make sense of. A search for his sister Emma, on the other hand, might help to locate the family in 1881.

As with other indexes, such as the General Register Office indexes, consider the possibility that the surname has been misspelt, misread or mis-transcribed and try a few variants.

If you cannot find your ancestor's name in an index you will have to try something else. The Findmypast website offers a useful address search which will highlight the names of people living in the same street. Also, before the advent of electronic indexing researchers went to certificates of birth, marriage and death or parish register entries to find an address. Using that address, and a map of the area, they searched through census images on microfilm, page by page, using the street indexes provided by the library or archive holding the microfilm, until they found the family they were looking for. That option, or the option of browsing through electronic images online, is still open to you. It has other advantages too. While you are searching you can note other people of the same surname living in the same location. Families often gathered together and lived near each other.

Using this method you can also get to know the kind of neighbourhood your ancestors lived in by looking at the occupations of the people they lived among. That is still possible using the digital images online, and some people still do it, but the temptation is always there to find what you are looking for and move on. However, the more you learn about each family grouping in its home setting, the better equipped you will be to move backwards towards the next generation.

1939 National Identity Survey

On the night of 29 September 1939, information about the population was gathered in preparation for the issue of National Identity Cards. On a sheet of paper resembling a short census form, people were asked for their name, date of birth, sex, marital status, occupation and whether they were a member of the armed forces or reserves. The National Health Service Information Centre will now provide this information on individuals in England and Wales, provided they are recorded as deceased. A form is available online and a fairly substantial non-refundable fee is payable. As in a census, only those who were in a particular household on the night in question were recorded. This might mean members of the Armed Forces were not listed at home, and it is said that some young men were missed out in the hope they would not be called up for National Service. More information from the NHS Information Centre at www.ic.nhs.uk.

In the Name of God Amen. The Nine & Twentyeth Day of September in ye Eight year
of ye Reigne of our Soveringe Lord George By ye Grace of God of Great Brittain ffrance
And Ireland King Defender of ye ffaith &c: Annoqz Domi 1721
I Job Barker of Starknes Lane in ye parish of Darly in ye County of Derby Weaver Being
But weak in body But of Good & perfect Memory Thankes be to Almighty God And Calling to
Remembrance ye Uncertain Estate of this Transitory Life And yt all fflesh must Yield unto Death whom
It shall please God to Call. Doe make Constitute ordaine & Declare this my Last Will & Testament
In manner & Form ffollowing Revoking & Annulling by these psents all other willy Testament
Heretofore by me made & Declared Either by word or writting & this to be taken for my Last will
And Testament & none other And first being penitent & sorry from ye Bottom of my heart for
My Sins past Most Humbly Desiring Forgiveness for ye Same I Give & Comit my Soul unto
Almighty God my Saviour & Redeemer in whom And by ye merits of Jesus Christ I Trust
And Believe assuredly to be Saved & to have full Forgiveness of all my Sins And yt my Soul
With my Body att ye General Day of Resurrection shall rise again with Joy And through the
Merits of Christs Death & passion. possess & inherit ye Kingdom of heaven prepared for his Elect
And Chosen & my Body to be Buried as my Executrix shall please and appoint And now for ye settling
of my Temporal Estate & such Goods Chattels & Debts as it hath pleased God far above my
Deserts to bestow upon me I doe order Give & Dispose ye Same in manner & form ffollowing
That is to say ffirst I will ye all those Debts and Dutyes as I owe in right or Conscience to any
Manner of person or persons whatsoever shall be well & truely paid & Contented or ordained to
Be paid within Convenient Time after my Decease by my Executrix hereafter named
Item I Give & Bequeath unto my Loving wife Elizabeth Barker one Cow one Heiffer Fifty Sheep
all my working Tools all money owing to me goods & Chattels whatsoever
Item I Give & Bequeath unto my Brother Samuel Barker all my Cloathes both woollen & Linning
Item I Give & Bequeath unto my Loving wife Elizabeth Barker all my personall Estate & Substance
Whatsoever what is not before Bequeathed Item I Doe hereby Nominate Constitute ordaine
And appoint my Loving wife my Executrix of This my Last will & Testament
Inwittness whereof I Job Barker have hereunto Set my hand & Seal ye Day & year
ffirst above written Annoqz Domi 1721
Sealed Signned Declared & publishhed to be ye
Last will & Testamt of ye above named Job Barker
And ye wittness subscribed their names in presence of
The Testator   And ye words (one Clark horse) was interlined &
     William martin   Before Sealing hereof

Job   ✕   Barker
      his mark

Poligene   ✕   Barker
Ler   mark
John I H Hollingworth
      his   Mark

Will of Job Barker of Darly [sic], Derbyshire, 1721. (Reproduced by permission of Lichfield Diocesan Record Office, Staffordshire ref. B/C/11.)

5 Wills and Letters of Administration

WILLS

Why do I need them?

A will can tell you all sorts of information about the family: how much money was left and how it was distributed. That is valuable information in its own right but, in its role as a legal document, a will had to give accurate information about who people were – and that is priceless to a family historian.

A will in England and Wales is usually signed by the person whose wishes it contains, and is witnessed by at least two people. It details how the person would like their possessions to be disposed of, usually to named family members, and appoints an executor or executors to carry out their wishes after their death. The executors may also be identified as family members. Every effort is made by those involved in writing the will to make sure the information in it is accurate and specific because if it is not, the will can be challenged in court.

When a person dies, having left a will, the executors named in the will usually have to apply to the courts for probate to be granted to enable them to carry out the wishes of the deceased. The court officials keep what is traditionally called an 'office copy'. It is these office copies that we usually see when we order a copy of a will.

What are my chances of finding my ancestor's will?

Not everyone made a will – probably only about ten per cent of the population in the mid-nineteenth century. However, it was not only the rich who made them. Even an agricultural labourer might make a will, particularly if he held 'copyhold' land under the manorial system (*see* Chapter 10). Soldiers and sailors often made wills. And a proportion of small businessmen and farmers would make them. Never assume that there will not be a will. See *Wills*

and Probate Records: A Guide for Family Historians by Karen Grannum and Nigel Taylor for more detail.

Women made fewer wills than men. According to figures for the year 1858 quoted in Grannum and Taylor, 5.6 per cent of women aged over twenty-one when they died that particular year left wills, with a further three per cent of women's estates going to administration. These women would be mostly spinsters and widows. At this time married women were excluded from making wills except with the permission of their husbands. Things did not change until 1882 when the Married Women's Property Act came into force. Other people who were not allowed to make wills included children and lunatics.

Sadly not all wills have survived, but it is always worth making the effort to look for them. Suggestions of where to look are given later in the chapter.

What can a Will tell me?

You will usually find a statement of the occupation of the person making the will, and an idea of where they lived. Their marital status and their state of health is generally made clear. The names of any children are often given, although the mention of 'all my children' without naming them can be frustrating. You should get an idea of the person's wealth from the items and money he or she is giving away (although sometimes people had inflated ideas of their own financial worth).

Wills, if you can find them, can give you detailed information about family members and the relationships between them. Those made before Civil Registration in 1837 and the national census coverage from 1841 can sometimes be the only confirmation of relationships found in Parish Registers. Wills are particularly useful in identifying individuals in families with common names. Furthermore, they can produce unexpected delights,

LETTERS OF ADMINISTRATION (ADMINISTRATIONS OR ADMONS)

If a person died without making a will, or if the will was in some way invalid, his family (or other people with an interest, such as creditors) could apply to the same authority that granted probate on wills to be granted Letters of Administration. These enabled the applicant to dispose of the deceased person's possessions in accordance with the inheritance laws prevailing at the time. Court officials kept 'office copies', as they did of wills, and it is these that you see when you apply for a copy of an administration.

Administrations – Why do I need them?

Letters of Administration, or 'admons' as they are known, usually contain less information than most wills and many people are tempted to ignore them. However, that can sometimes be a mistake. They can give you, at the very least, a date of death or a date before which the person died. An occupation for the deceased is often mentioned, and the people applying for administration are often relatives and are identified as such, with information about their occupations.

The search for wills and administrations divides clearly into two parts – those that went to probate or administration before 1858 and those after 1858. The example of an admon shown is the administration of the estate of Thomas Henry Skrine, who died before 1858 but whose Letters of Administration were granted after 1858.

The Probate Calendar of 1863 listing Thomas Henry Skrine Esquire gives quite a bit of information about him and his family. It tells us:

- The date when Letters of Administration were applied for – 4 August 1863.
- The name, date and place of death of the deceased (15 August 1815 at Madras in the East Indies) and the fact that he was a bachelor.
- The value of his estate (under £1500).
- The name, address and occupation of the Rev. Harcourt Skrine, applying for the letters of administration.
- The fact that the money left in the estate was to be for the 'Use and Benefit' of Isabella Skrine, and that

she was the spinster sister of the deceased and one of his next of kin.

If letters of administration had been applied for just after the death of Thomas Henry Skrine, under the church instead of under the civil system, there would have been far less information in the Calendars. However, when we look at the administration document itself we learn a great deal more:

- That the Rev. Harcourt Skrine was the nephew of the deceased.
- That Thomas Henry Skrine's parents might have been dead when he died and were certainly thought to be dead by 1863.
- That Isabella Skrine was of unsound mind (a fact unlikely to have emerged anywhere else).
- That there were two other siblings John Harcourt Skrine and Henrietta Skrine who, by 1863, were the 'only other next of kin of the said intestate being dead...'

That is a lot of additional family information from one administration document. It has to be admitted that they are not all like that – but it is a demonstration that they can be extremely useful and should not be ignored.

It can pay to keep looking

The administration or 'admon' opposite is also a very good example of how it can pay to keep looking for a will or administration. Normally people would look in the Calendars or indexes for five or ten years after someone's death in the hope of finding something. After that, the chances of a find diminish. However, it sometimes happens that a will or administration comes to light when someone else in the family dies, or if a financial need means that someone has to 'sort everything out'. This is what appears to have happened here because under the same date in the Probate Calendar, letters of administration were also applied for by the Rev. Harcourt Skrine for another sister of Isabella Skrine – Catharine Skrine who died in 1814 at Walton-on-Thames, before her brother Thomas Henry. The proceeds were also granted for the 'Use and Benefit' of Isabella Skrine Spinster.'

Administration.

Extracted by *Lomer & Co., Proctors, Doctors Commons.*

In Her Majesty's Court of Probate.

BE IT KNOWN, that on the *fourth* — day of *August* 18*63*, Letters of Administration of all and singular the personal estate and effects of

Thomas Henry Skrine late of Madras in the East Indies Esquire

deceased, who died on *the fifth day of August 1815,* at *Madras aforesaid a Bachelor without Parent and* intestate, were granted by Her Majesty's Court of Probate to *The Reverend Harcourt Skrine Clerk the lawful Nephew and one of the next of kin of Isabella Skrine Spinster (a person of unsound mind) the natural and lawful Sister and one of the next of kin of the said intestate for the use and benefit of the said Isabella Skrine and during her unsoundness of mind he the said Reverend Harcourt Skrine* of the said intestate, — having been first sworn well and faithfully to administer the same, by paying the just debts of the said intestate, and distributing the residue *of his estate and effects* according to law, and to exhibit a true and perfect inventory of all and singular the said estate and effects, and to render a just and true account thereof whenever required by law so to do. *John Harcourt Skrine and Henrietta Skrine Spinster the natural and lawful Brother and Sister also and only other next of kin of the said intestate being dead.*

A. F. Bayford
Registrar

Sworn under One thousand five hundred pounds.

Executor's copy of Letters of Administration of the Effects of Thomas Henry Skrine 1863. (Crown Copyright. Reproduced under the terms of the Click-Use Licence.)

How do I obtain copies of Wills or Letters of Administration dated after 1858?

You can go in person to the Principal Probate Registry or your nearest District Probate Registry and fill in a form and pay the fee. You will receive your copy within a few days. You can also apply by post, either by letter or by completing a form available online at the website of the Principal Probate Registry. Enclose a cheque or postal order in payment of the fee. Current fees can be found on the website.

Applying for a search to be done for you

If you are unable to consult the Calendars/Indexes you can apply to the Probate Registry for a search to be done on your behalf. Give them as much information as you can, preferably from the death certificate.

Terms relating to Church of England structure and Church Courts

Parish: administered by a vicar, rector or perpetual curate, all also known as the 'incumbent'.

Deanery: a group of parishes overseen by a rural dean. Rural deans in the PCY sometimes dealt with probate but it was not normally done in the PCC.

Archdeaconry: a division within a diocese, consisting of several deaneries and administered by an archdeacon.

Diocese: a large area, consisting of several archdeaconries and overseen by a bishop, often conforming roughly to county boundaries.

Episcopal Consistory Court: a court covering a diocese, overseen by a bishop.

Episcopal Commissary Court: a court covering an area of a diocese, also overseen by a bishop.

Peculiar: a small self-governing area exempt from the authority of an archdeacon or bishop. The Peculiar was able, among other things, to grant probate or letters of administration.

Archdiocese: The largest area covered by one church court. For the period while church courts were dealing with probate it was one of only two provinces of York and Canterbury, covering the North and South of the country respectively. There were only two Prerogative Courts – Canterbury and York.

Send your request to The Postal Searches and Copies Department, The Probate Registry, Castle Chambers, Clifford Street, York YO1 9RG.

Wills and Administrations before 1858

Before 1858 Wills were proved in the Church Courts of the Church of England. There were quite a lot of them, which can make the thought of searching for wills at this period a bit daunting but there are some very good finding aids available.

Church Courts

There were different layers of Church Courts. These roughly corresponded to the layers of the hierarchy of the Church of England – from the lowest, local Archdeaconry courts and those of Peculiars (*see* box) to the Prerogative Courts of Canterbury and York, the highest courts available for the purpose of proving Wills or applying for Letters of Administration.

The Prerogative Court of Canterbury (PCC) covered the Southern Province, under the Archbishop of Canterbury – that is most of the Midlands, the South of England and most of Wales. The PCC also had over-riding jurisdiction for England and Wales, including the area covered by the Prerogative Court of York.

The Prerogative Court of York (PCY) covered the Northern counties of Cheshire, Cumberland, Durham, Lancashire, Northumberland, Nottinghamshire (until the mid-1800s), Westmorland, Yorkshire and the Isle of Man.

Which court would have dealt with my ancestor's will?

There is a fairly logical route to follow which states that if the deceased had property within a small area (that is the boundaries of one archdeaconry or within a peculiar) then their executors were most likely to have gone to one of these local level courts to prove the will. If their property fell within more than one archdeaconry then the diocese would be the place to look as this is the next level up. The two archdioceses of Canterbury and York were the next step, with Canterbury having overall authority. People who died abroad generally had their wills proved at the Prerogative Court of Canterbury, so look here first for wills of soldiers and sailors in particular. Executors of wealthier

WILLS AND LETTERS OF ADMINISTRATION   67

people, or those who had standing in society, might have gone to the PCC even if they did not really need to.

Where do I go for a copy of a will for England and Wales before 1858?

Prerogative Court of Canterbury

Nowadays it is very tempting to start a search at the top, with the PCC wills, because they are indexed online at the National Archives' Documents Online website, and it is fairly easy to eliminate them from your enquiries. There is a charge for copies but they can be seen free at the National Archives (series PROB11). Some Royal Navy (1786–1882) wills are also in Documents Online in series ADM48.

The copy wills available online in series PROB11 are not the original wills. They are office copies entered into a book at or near the time of probate. Original wills, providing they have survived, are at the National Archives at Kew in series PROB10. Reasons for looking in PROB10 include finding an original signature, checking a fact from the copy or searching for a will that was not registered in PROB11.

The online index to PCC wills does not include letters of administration. There are indexes, some printed, to PCC administrations but they vary in type and availability. There are published indexes 1559–1660, which you might find in larger libraries and archives. There are also other indexes and calendars available covering the whole period up to 1858 at the National Archives including two sets of A4 folders on the shelves containing indexes 1700–1800. The Society of Genealogists has an index 1750–1800.

Prerogative Court of York

These wills are held at the Borthwick Institute for Historical Research in York (*see* The Borthwick Institute website in the list at the back) and the Origins Network (*see* website list) has the Prerogative and Exchequer Court of York Probate Index online. You can search the index for the name you are looking for and take a note of the Borthwick Institute reference number for the original. Copies can be ordered online, or by post from the Borthwick Institute.

Wills from the lower Church Courts

These are scattered around the country, usually in county archives. Most county archives are also the diocesan archives for the Church of England, holding the Church's records for the diocese, so it is a good idea to make contact with the county archive first. If the diocesan archive is separate, the county archive will tell you where it is.

Phillimore's Atlas and Index of Parish Registers has parish maps for each county which also show the Church courts with jurisdiction over each parish. There is a copy on the reference shelves of most archives. So you can look at the map, identify the parish where you think your ancestor's property might have been located, and then look for the coloured band surrounding that area on the map. The key to the different colours will tell you which courts were available to the executors and with that information in mind you can contact the county archive to ask if they hold the wills and administrations for that particular court. There is a useful list of courts for each county in John Richardson's *The Local Historian's Encyclopaedia*. Jeremy Gibson and Else Churchill's *Probate Jurisdictions: Where to Look for Wills* is a comprehensive guide to where you might find them.

The Civil War and Interregnum

Between around 1643 and 1660 – while the Civil War was in full swing and during the Commonwealth (Interregnum) when Oliver Cromwell was in charge – wills were generally written in English instead of Latin. For most of that period they were supposed to have been proved by a Parliamentary court in London but actually it was a bit of a muddle. Some wills were not proved until after 1660, and some not at all. Those that were proved have mostly been incorporated into the PCC wills so it is there that you should look first for a will during that period.

People did not always follow the 'rules'

Probate was not always granted in the area where your ancestor lived. You might have to look further afield. The court used depended on where the deceased person's property was – not where they were when they died.

People did not always do what you might expect. Some wealthy families preferred to use a higher court, usually the PCC, perhaps for the sake of privacy. Also an executor in the north of England might choose to go to the PCY, for example, if it was more convenient for him to travel to York than to the archdeaconry court where the deceased held his property. As long as all the deceased's property was within the Northern Province he was entitled to do this. If the deceased held Government Stocks, however, the executor would have to go to London.

How do I read an old will?

Don't be put off looking for wills by the fact that they might contain old handwriting and some Latin. Latin ceased to be used as the legal language in 1733 but you can get quite a long way back in time before coming across any Latin at all, and then sometimes only the probate part of the will may be in Latin (see page 70). Probate is usually in a recognizable form of words that you should be able to decipher with the help of a good Latin primer such as *A Latin Glossary for Family and Local Historians* by Janet Morris.

When you look at the old handwriting, try to take it

Where do I look for wills proved in Wales?

Post-1858 wills for Wales are included in the National Probate Calendars/Indexes, so you will find them in the same way as you would find a will for England. Welsh Wills before 1858, if they are not to be found in the records of the PCC, are most likely to be in the National Library of Wales, Aberystwyth. Over 190,000 Welsh wills are available to view free online at their website. They charge for copies but you can look at them free.

The counties whose original wills have been deposited at the National Library of Wales are:
- Bangor: 1635–1858
- Brecon: 1543–1858
- Chester (Welsh wills): 1557–1858
- Hawarden: 1554–1858
- Llandaf: 1568–1857
- St Asaph: 1565–1857
- St David's: 1556–1858

(List by kind permission of the National Library of Wales)

slowly. You will get better at it with practice. It is usually possible to get a photocopy of an old will that you are interested in, so you can take it home and work on it.

If you then decide to transcribe it there are a number of things to bear in mind:
- When transcribing an old document, transcribe it exactly as it is written.
- When a new line begins, start a new line of the transcription (numbering the lines can be a good idea).
- If you cannot make out a word, leave a gap noting how many words or letters you think are missing.
- There are some recognizable abbreviations. If you find an abbreviated word expand it and put the expanded letters in square brackets. The most common mistake is copying down 'Ye' for 'the'. Although it looks like a letter Y it is in fact the way that 'th' was written.
- If you don't recognize a letter, look for words you are sure about further down and see if you can match the letter that way. Do not make it up – you need to be able to rely on what you have written, and there is no disgrace if you cannot read it as long as you make a note that is capable of being understood.
- Don't try to read the document in the same way that you would normally read a letter or your notes, because your eye will fill in with information that is not there. Look at it a letter or a word at a time until you are more practised.

The same advice applies to reading any old document, including parish registers.

The National Archives have some excellent examples of old handwriting that you can practise on. Go to their website and look for the palaeography tutorials. There are also some very useful books. Hilda E. P. Grieve's *Examples of English Handwriting 1150–1750* gives a lot of different examples. Alf Ison's *A Secretary Hand ABC Book* treats each letter individually, with possible variants.

The National Archives website also has an excellent guide to the Latin used in documents between 1086 and 1733. If you do come across an old will in Latin, and you are fairly certain that it relates to your family, it might also be worth enquiring about having a translation done. The Association of Genealogists and Researchers in

Examples of handwriting

Gets some practice in reading old handwriting by looking at the wills on pages 60 and 70.

Handwriting

A 'c' that looks like an 'r'

An 'r' that dips in the middle

A double 'f' for a single capital 'F'

Abbreviations

'the' looks as though it is written as 'ye'

'that', still with the same symbol for 'th', is written 'yt'

'&' for '&c' (etc.) and for 'and'

A symbol like a cartoon 'thought bubble' represents 're' here. Often found at the end of a word for 'er', here it is used in the middle

A line above a letter shows a letter is missing. Strictly, a straight line signifies one letter, a wavy line for more

A line through the letter 'p' shows a missing 'er'

Using these clues, you should be able to manage to read most of the words in both wills.

Archives website gives professional researchers who offer translation.

Wills not proved

Many wills were never proved, or granted probate. Some families would not bother about probate if they all agreed on how things were to be divided. Going to probate cost money. Or a will would be drawn up and never signed. Some of these wills might still lie undiscovered in solicitors' papers. (*See* Chapter 10 for ways of accessing solicitors' papers.)

Disputed wills

The National Archives has papers from some disputes over wills in the Court of Probate and Supreme Court of Judicature in series J121. Some documents exhibited in court are in J90. Both are searchable by name in the National Archives catalogue. Cases in the Court of Chancery can also be searched in the catalogue by name.

Where do I go from here?

The date that the will was signed gives you a date at which it is reasonable to assume that the people named in the will were alive. You can find the married names of daughters of the family, usually with the occupation of their husbands and sometimes with an idea of where they lived. From there you can look for a marriage knowing that it occurred before the date the will was signed. Younger family members are often remembered with the provision that they would receive their inheritance on reaching the age of twenty-one. This tells you that they were still under twenty-one on the date the will was signed. This may all seem very obvious but when you are struggling with early parish registers holding only basic information it is the equivalent of gold dust and gives you some useful limits to your search for births, baptisms, marriages and deaths.

If you find a will, note every relationship mentioned and every name – even those you don't recognize. If a legal settlement or another will is mentioned, go in search of those documents as well.

DEATH DUTY REGISTERS

If you have a will or letters of administration granted between 1796 and 1903 you should think about consulting the Death Duty Registers in case tax was payable on the estate. Death Duty Registers are a Government record of taxes levied on the estates of people who had died – Estate Duty, Legacy Duty and Succession Duty.

Why do I need them?

Death Duty Registers were an ongoing record of what happened to a person's estate after probate. Up to 1853 tax was only payable on personal estate over a certain value, not so-called 'real estate' or property, so the idea you might get of someone's wealth will not necessarily be accurate. However, the beauty of these registers is

Nuncupative or spoken will of Elizabeth Bee of Rudgely [sic], Staffordshire 1676. (Reproduced by permission of Lichfield Diocesan Record Office, Staffordshire ref P/C/11.)

that they were revisited by officials, sometimes years after the death, when something of note happened, for example the death of an heir or the births of children or grandchildren after the date of death. This was noted on the record. If you are lucky you can find information about a person's heirs long after he or she had died and their property was disposed of.

Where can I find them?
Death Duty Registers are kept at the National Archives at Kew in series IR26. Some are available online at their Documents Online website. You can see the full range at the National Archives.

You can also consult the indexes to the Death Duty Registers 1796–1903 online at Findmypast to see if an

Wills: Clues from the language

A will that begins with the word Memorandum or Memoranda is a spoken will often dictated at a person's death bed. The name for this type of will is a 'nuncupative' will. After 1837 the only type of nuncupative will that was accepted by the courts was one made by a soldier or sailor while on active service but before that time it is quite easy to come across one.

Many older wills, like the will of Job Barker, weaver, of Darly [sic] in Derbyshire illustrated at the beginning of this chapter, begin with the words 'In the Name of God Amen' or 'In Dei Nomine Amen' and will continue with words committing the testator's soul to God and giving instructions as to how they want to be buried. The words 'weak in Body but of Good and perfect Memory' are important because they state that he has the mental capacity to make the will. This part of the will can also give a hint as to a person's religious affiliation. Mention of the Virgin Mary might, for example, mean the deceased had Catholic leanings; a request for a simple inexpensive burial might come from a nonconformist. This could influence where you start looking for a burial or for other events in the person's life.

Another clue to look out for – members of the Society of Friends, commonly known as Quakers, did not use the names of days of the week or months of the year because they were based on the names of pagan gods. Wills of Quakers are likely to use phrases such as 'the third month' and 'the second day'. Don't confuse this with the form of date given as a 'regnal year', which reads something like 'the third year in the reign of our Lord and Sovereign King Henry.' This is quite normal in early wills and is often followed by a recognizable date, as in the will of Job Barker. If not, there are lists of regnal years in many almanacs and specialist books including John Richardson's *The Local Historian's Encyclopaedia*.

There was a period when Catholics were not allowed to make wills so some of these can come heavily disguised. Michael Gandy, in his book *Tracing your Catholic Ancestry in England*, quotes the mention of a bequest to a 'Mr Dowey for purposes he knows of...'; code in a Catholic will for a bequest to the well-known Catholic school at Douai in Northern France to which some wealthier English Catholics sent their offspring.

Family relationships are usually clearly spelled out but some were not as clearly defined as they are today. Remember that a 'cousin' was not necessarily a first cousin, often being used to describe a more distant relation; a 'sister' or 'sister-in-law' might be a step-sister and a 'mother-in-law' could conceivably be a step-mother. A 'niece' or 'nephew' might even turn out to be a grandchild.

Job Barker's will is relatively easy to read. Take it slowly, a line at a time, and see what you can make of it. The word 'Item' appears when a new bequest or instruction is introduced. He appoints his wife Elizabeth as Executrix. She is the main beneficiary, along with his brother Samuel.

For more advice on reading and transcribing old documents, see above.

---

entry has survived for your ancestor. The original indexes are in the National Archives in series IR27.

The indexes can also be useful if you are struggling to find a will, although they only include wills that were subject to death duty. They name the church court where the will was proved. The index is not entirely searchable electronically. Images of several original, handwritten indexes have to be searched to cover one year. Origins Network is currently building an electronic index to pre-1858 wills, so keep an eye on the website.

Reading Death Duty Registers

When you get to the Death Duty Registers they are full of abbreviations and notes that are not understandable to ordinary mortals. However, the National Archives has produced a very good research guide to the abbreviations and the layout. This is available online or at the National Archives. There is also a very helpful chapter on Death Duty Registers in Grannum and Taylor's *Wills and Probate Records – A Guide for Family Historians*.

BAPTISMS solemnized in the Parish of *Saint Martin in Birmingham* in the County of *Warwick in January* in the Year 18*13*

When Baptized.	Child's Christian Name.	Parents Name.		Abode.	Quality, Trade, or Profession.	By whom the Ceremony was performed.
		Christian.	Surname.			
1813. January 25th No. 105.	James Son of Born Dec. 3d 1810	James Mary	Thompson	Deretend	Black Smith	Wm Johnson
25th No. 106.	Charles Son of Born Aug 6th 1812	James Mary	Thompson	Deretend	Black Smith	Wm Johnson
25th No. 107.	Sophia Daur of Born May 6th 1812	James Margaret	Rose	Livery Street	Serjeant	Wm Johnson
25th No. 108.	Frederick Son of Born Mar 3d 1810	John Rebecca	Sargeant	Bishop gate Street	Gilt Toy Maker	Wm Johnson
25th No. 109.	Caroline Daur of Born Jany 15th 1812	John Rebecca	Sargeant	Bishop gate Street	Gilt Toy Maker	Wm Johnson
26th No. 110.	Ann Daur of	John Elizabeth	Fisher	Bordsley Street	Sawyer	Wm Johnson
26th No. 111.	Charles Son of Born Dec. 91 1812	James Miriam	Lonsdale	Bartholomew Street	Supervisor	Wm Johnson
26th No. 112.	Deodatus Son of	Deodatus Elizabeth	Carr	Bull Ring	Druggist	Wm Johnson

Baptisms at the Parish Church of St Martin, Birmingham 1813. (Reproduced with the permission of Birmingham Libraries and Archives ref. DRO/34/9 p14 and the Rector and Churchwardens of St Martin in the Bull Ring.)

6 Parish Registers and Marriage Licences, Indexes and Bishops' Transcripts

PARISH REGISTERS

Why do I need them?

Before civil registration started in 1837, and gave us the certificates of birth, marriage and death that we use today, the chief way of registering life's major events was through the Church of England registers of baptism, marriage and burial. This makes these registers the most consistent and widely available source of vital information before 1837. They are also invaluable after 1837 because you can use them to check against the information in the available census returns every ten years from 1841 to 1911 and to help you locate certificates of birth, marriage and death and other evidence up to the present day.

How do I use them?

Once you start using parish registers as your main source of information, for research before 1837, the way you actually do the research has to change a little. You no longer have census returns (*see* Chapter 4) to make your life easier by giving you more information about where a person has come from and where they went. If your ancestor has a common name you might find yourself looking at two or three people in the same parish and wondering which of them is 'yours'.

The only way round this is to take biographical notes about each of them, and their families, and hope that eventually you will be able to eliminate the others from your enquiries. The most valuable help to you in this can come, not only from parish registers, but from bishops' transcripts, marriage licences, wills (*see* Chapter 5) and the so-called 'parish chest' documents (*see* Chapter 8).

How do I find my ancestor in parish registers?

Most people start by doing it the easy way, looking at the many indexes now available online or in archives and public libraries. If they do not find what they are looking for in the indexes they go to the original registers, on microfilm, microfiche or increasingly online.

Whatever index you might use to try to find the baptism, marriage or burial of your ancestor – always confirm anything you find by looking at the original entry in the parish register. It might give you more information, or it might show up an error in the transcription of the information into the index. Either way, you need to see it.

Many names appearing in those parish registers are not included in indexes and you should try to identify the parishes that are not in the indexes and search through the original registers if they belong to a parish that might be relevant to your family. Use your common sense – if your family names suddenly appear from the indexes to have moved to a place many miles away from where you have been locating them thus far, it is highly probable that the family is not in the indexes and the people you have found are not your family at all. In any case you will need to do some thorough searching of the original registers and other sources to prove that they are, indeed, your ancestors and to find out when they moved.

When people did move, they often did not move far

Dates for Parish Registers

1538: during the reign of Henry VIII it was decided that a record should be kept of baptisms, marriages and burials in each Parish 'to avoid disputes touching ages, titles, or lineal descents, and whether anyone was the King's born subject or not...'. *

1598: from this date the registers were to be written on parchment instead of paper. Paper deteriorated too quickly, so all entries to date were supposed to be copied into a new parchment register. Many parishes only did this back to the start of the reign of their current Queen – Elizabeth I in 1558. Once a year a transcript of the parish register had to be sent to the Bishop.

1645: during the 'Commonwealth Period', when Oliver Cromwell was in charge, he appointed his own officials to register births, marriages and deaths. Many of these records have not survived. The Civil War had already disrupted the keeping of records so be prepared to find very little during and around the fifteen years roughly from 1645 to 1660. Those records that do survive should be found in county record offices. Once 'normal service' had been resumed from 1660 some entries were made in parish registers relating to events during the period and some late baptisms were performed.

1666 and 1678: in order to boost the wool trade, it was decreed that everyone who was buried should be buried in a woollen shroud. Each time someone, usually a relative, had to swear an affidavit that this had been done. You might find the note 'Affid.' next to a burial, declaring this. The practice gradually died out during the eighteenth century and the law was repealed in the early nineteenth century.

1695: a short-lived attempt was made to levy charges for the recording in the register of baptisms, marriages and burials. Look out for a rush of late baptisms after the charges were lifted in 1706.

1751–2: calendar change. Up to and from this date you can find the year given as two possible dates, for example 1751/2 for entries at the beginning of January. This year marked the change in England and Wales from the Julian Calendar to the Gregorian Calendar. Until 1752 each new year had started on 25 March but from 1752 onwards each new year started on 1 January. In addition an adjustment was made to bring England into line with other countries' calendars. This involved losing eleven days out of the month of September, but only for one year.

1753: Hardwicke's Marriage Act. Set procedures for marriages were introduced as a reaction to the increasing number of clandestine marriages. Banns (a notice that it was intended for the marriage to take place) were to be read in church for three weeks before the marriage. A residential qualification was introduced. Signatures of witnesses and of the bride and groom were kept in the new, separate marriage register. Jews and Quakers were exempt from this. All other marriages had to take place in a Church of England, performed by an Anglican clergyman, in order to be regarded as legal.

1783: the Stamp Act – this was another attempt to introduce charges for registering baptisms, marriages and burials in the Parish Register. People might have thought twice before baptising their children or marrying. The Stamp Act was repealed after ten years.

1812: new registers were introduced with a set form of baptism recording place of residence and father's occupation. The set form of burial recording gives age at death and place of residence.

1837: parish registers change to reflect the form of marriage certificate introduced by the start of civil registration, giving ages and occupations for the couple, names and occupations of their fathers and a place of residence for the bride and groom. Signatures of witnesses were still included.

* 'Henry VIII: December 1538 26-31', *Letters and Papers, Foreign and Domestic, Henry VIII, Volume 13 Part 2: August–December 1538* (1893), pp. 475-496.

away. If you cannot find them in the parish you expected, simply widen your search to neighbouring parishes. Look at one of the county maps published by the Institute of Heraldic and Genealogical Studies or in *Phillimore's Atlas and Index of Parish Registers* (ed. C. Humphery-Smith) to see how the parishes in a particular county sit next to each other. A thorough search will include both indexes and a combination of parish maps and original registers.

Whatever search you are doing, keep a careful note of the page numbers and the dates you have searched between. Also the registers you have consulted, and where you saw them. Make a note of exactly what you were looking for – instances of a particular surname, or a combination of forename and surname. You will not remember a few days later when you look at your notes.

WHAT CAN PARISH REGISTERS TELL ME?

Baptism registers tell the date of baptism, not the date of birth. If you are lucky both dates might be included, as on page 72, but it is not generally the case. Likewise burial registers give the date of burial – not of death, unless it is included as additional information. Marriage registers give the date of the marriage and might indicate whether banns were called or a licence applied for. Sometimes separate banns registers were kept.

It is important to remember that early parish registers, in particular, were not necessarily written up at the time of the event. The incumbent (a term used to describe the parish priest, rector or vicar) would often write details down on scraps of paper to be entered into the register later – or even commit them to memory. That could explain some gaps in baptism entries where the child's name is not present, or the forename of a parent might be missing.

In the early days, as a general rule, everything went in one General Register. Later, marriage registers became separate and baptisms and burials were listed in their own registers at least from 1812. A lot depended on the individual incumbent as to how things were laid out and how much information was included.

The introduction of a formal layout for parish registers did a lot to help researchers in terms of information about individuals but some of the early registers contained additional information that was largely lost in

the days after form-filling was introduced. Reports on harvests, the weather, the coronations of kings and queens – even drawings – could appear in amongst the baptisms, marriages and burials and add valuable insights into the everyday lives of our ancestors. The incumbent might even comment about the parishioners themselves – not all of it complimentary! The example on page 76 from the parish of Alrewas in Staffordshire goes into great detail about the harsh winter of 1794–5 and the damage done to the bridges in the area by the thaw that followed. That kind of information became much more scarce after 1812.

Baptism

Baptism, in the main, took place a few days after the birth, particularly in the early years when a larger proportion of children died in infancy. However, a number of children slipped through the net and were baptized late. Unless the age is given, the only clue to this you are likely to get is if a whole family were baptized together or, perhaps, if the parish priest decided to round up the children living in his parish who had been missed. In these cases you would get a mass of baptisms on one day and occasionally the date of birth might be given. So if you find a baptism in an index that looks a little later than the one you were looking for, it is always worth searching for the original entry. A very late, adult baptism might also occur just prior to a marriage if it was found that one of the parties had not been baptised previously. If it is not shown to be a late or adult baptism by the information given in the register you cannot assume it to be so.

Baptism entries before 1812 are likely to be written on a single line beginning or ending with the date. As a bare minimum you are likely to find the name of the child and of the father. The mother's forename might also be included and, with luck, the father's occupation and even a place of residence. Do be careful – in a so-called 'General Register' the baptisms and burials are often listed on the same page. It is very easy for the eye to slip from a 'bap' to a 'bur' noted down the side. Also, always check up to a year at least after the baptism (more to be on the safe side) for an infant burial of the same child. There is little point in looking for a marriage if the poor

Burials at the Parish Church of All Saints, Alrewas, Staffordshire 1795. (Reproduced by permission of Staffordshire Record Office ref F783/1/1/3 and the Vicar and Churchwardens of All Saints, Alrewas.)

Age at marriage

During the seventeenth and eighteenth centuries people, on average, married in their mid-twenties. It was not unusual for the bride to be pregnant or even to have had a baby before the marriage. It is also important to remember that until 1929 a legal marriage could take place at age fourteen for a boy and twelve for a girl. This was comparatively rare but if you are missing a marriage it might be worth considering this possibility.

Calendar changes

In 1752 England and Wales went through a calendar change to bring them in line with the rest of Western Europe. The change was from the so-called Julian calendar to the Gregorian calendar. In effect before 1752 the year had begun on 25 March and there were differences in dates between countries which led to odd things apparently happening, such as the instance quoted by Bevan when 'William of Orange...left Holland on 11th November 1688, to arrive in England on 5th November' [see p16, *Tracing Your Ancestors in the Public Record Office* by Amanda Bevan]. After the change, the year number changed on 1 January. In addition, in 1752 itself, eleven days disappeared from the month of September to bring the numbering of the days into line with the rest of Europe.

You will probably find dates in the early months of the year given in the form 20 January 1751–2, meaning 1751 in the old style of calendar but 1752 in the new. If you do find this, take a note of the date exactly as it is written so that you will be able to make a judgement further down the line as to what the date entailed.

child was already dead! And a high proportion of children did die before their fifth birthday.

Baptism entries after 1812 are quite informative because they are on a standard form. Apart from the date, they usually give the forenames of both parents, where they lived and the father's surname and occupation. The only people who might regret the introduction of the 1812 format are researchers in the Diocese of York. Thanks to the so-called Dade Registers, introduced in much of the Diocese in 1777, they already had a mine of information with each baptism entry, including names of grandparents and even great-grandparents. Sponsors or godparents might be named in later ones. A handful of other English counties brought in a similar system later but it was, sadly, very short-lived.

Marriage

Marriage entries up to 1754 often simply give the names of the bride and groom and the date. Additional information might, if you were lucky, include the name of the parish where one of them came from if he or she was not from the parish where the marriage was taking place. Just because a different parish of origin for one or both of the parties is not mentioned, it cannot be taken as a certainty that both bride and groom had lived a long time in the parish where they married. However, that is the obvious place to start looking for other clues. Sometimes if a marriage licence had been obtained, there might be 'Lic' written by the entry. Much depended on the thoroughness of the person writing up the register.

After 1754 a form was introduced which allowed

more information to be included: for instance, the parish of origin of the bride and groom and whether the marriage took place after banns or by licence. Also included were the signatures or marks of the parties and the signatures of at least two witnesses to the ceremony. Always note down the names of witnesses – they might be family members. However, take care also to look at the entries each side of the one you are interested in. If the same witnesses appear on several dates during the register it is likely that they were church officials or close neighbours of the church dragged in on occasions when no family and friends were present.

After civil registration was introduced in 1837, the pages in the marriage register would take the same form as the registers held by local registrars (see Chapter 2). The church's copy of the register would usually be signed at the time of the ceremony and is a good place to look for an original signature of your ancestor. Copies of marriage certificates obtained from the General Register

Marriages at the Parish Church of St Martin, Birmingham 1802, showing two by banns and two by licence. (Reproduced with the permission of Birmingham Libraries and Archives ref. DRO/34/33 p4 and the Rector and Churchwardens of St Martin in the Bull Ring.)

Office should contain the same information but will be copies made at a later date.

MARRIAGE BY BANNS

Banns were usually called in church over three Sundays before the anticipated date of the marriage in order to give adequate public notice of a couple's intention to marry. This was intended to allow objections to be raised to the marriage, perhaps to prevent someone marrying twice. If the bride and groom lived in different parishes banns were read in both.

Sometimes separate registers were kept for banns. They are always worth looking for in case they contain additional information. There were occasions when banns were read and no marriage was recorded. Banns registers are rarely indexed so you would have to search the original or a microfilm copy.

MARRIAGE BY LICENCE

If you find a marriage by licence in a parish register (see the first two marriages entered on page 78) you should follow it up by trying to find the application for the licence because it is possible you might find some extremely useful, additional information about your ancestors.

If a couple wanted to avoid the calling of banns over three weeks it was open to them to apply to their local church authorities for a licence. This was not a so-called 'special licence' of which there were very few, usually only available to the rich. This was a licence available to all as long as they had, until 1823, someone to help them to underwrite it with a financial guarantee or bond. They also had to swear an affidavit or 'allegation' that they were telling the truth about their freedom to marry. There were many possible reasons for marrying by licence – if the groom was a soldier leaving immediately to join his regiment; if the bride was pregnant and the parish authorities wanted to be sure the father did not abscond before marrying her, leaving her dependent on the parish; if either the bride or groom was non-conformist (see Chapter 7); if one of the parties was a minor; if the marriage was due to take place during Lent or simply because it was thought to confer a sort of social status.

Some of the papers relating to marriage by licence survive in county archives. Those county archives that do not also have safe-keeping of the old records of the local diocese of the Church of England will be able to tell you where they are. The bonds and allegations are most likely to have survived. The licences themselves, having been handed over to the parties involved, are usually long gone. Some marriage bonds for Wales from 1661 are in the National Library of Wales in Aberystwyth.

What can applications for a marriage licence tell me?

The kind of additional information you might find in the bonds and allegations includes the ages of the bride and groom, the occupation of the groom, the names and occupations of those guaranteeing the bond (there is a strong possibility that these will be relatives) and the parish of origin of either the bride or groom. Some archives have alphabetical indexes to their marriage bonds and allegations. In others it will be necessary to go and search through a box or folder sorted by the year of the marriage. In either case the possible prize is well worth the effort.

Burial

Burial entries in early registers can often be found on the same page as baptisms, so you might have to concentrate hard to extract them. Sometimes they consist solely of a date and a name but if you are lucky an age might be given. The burial of a child might not be distinguished from that of an adult but the words 'daughter of...' or 'son of...' will sometimes help you to identify them.

Most people were buried near to where they died which can lead to difficulties in finding particularly a pre-1837 death and burial of a soldier or traveller. The expense and logistics of moving a body back to the home parish would mean this was not an option for most people.

The word 'Affid' next to a burial entry is an indication that the seventeenth-century rules regarding the process of burial in a woollen shroud had been followed (see 'Dates for Parish Registers' on page 74). If the rules were not followed a payment had to be made. The practice seems to have been observed with varying amounts of rigour, perhaps more so in areas where wool was an important source of income. Some parishes kept separate registers for 'burials in woollen'; some did not note it at all.

The introduction of civil registration in 1837 can be helpful in finding a burial. Once you have a death certificate with a date of death it is usual to find a burial, somewhere local to the place of death, taking place within a few days. An inquest might delay things a little, but you would get an indication from the death certificate that an inquest was likely to have taken place (*see* Chapter 2).

You might have a more difficult search on your hands for a burial in a city than a burial in a small town or village. By the beginning of the nineteenth century the burial grounds of churches in many towns and cities were getting full. Some stopped taking burials altogether, except additions to family tombs. Municipal burial grounds developed roughly from this time onwards (*see* Chapter 11). If you cannot find a burial at all, but have a date of death, try the newspapers (*see* Chapter 3) for an obituary, a death announcement or report of the funeral. There is always the possibility that the mortal remains were used in the furtherance of medical science, but it is difficult to prove. It is probably more likely that the priest performing the ceremony lost the scrap of paper on which he had noted the details and forgot to enter it into the register. During the twentieth century more and more people also opted for cremation (*see* Chapter 11).

Where can I find Parish Registers?

You will probably not be allowed to see the fragile original parish registers but microfilm and fiche or electronic images of parish registers will be available at the county archive for the county where your ancestor lived. Many county archives are also Diocesan Record Offices keeping the day-to-day administrative archives for the Church of England diocese too, so you might also be able to access Bishops' Transcripts, Marriage Licences and Wills dated before 1858 (*see* Chapter 5). It is always a good idea to telephone or look at the website to check opening hours before visiting any archive. If registers are on microfilm or microfiche you would need to book a microfilm or microfiche reader in advance to be sure of being able to view the items you want. If, as in Staffordshire, the

Always consult the original register

No matter how good the transcript or the index is, there is no excuse for not consulting the original register whether on microfilm or fiche, or an electronic image. Distance need not be a bar. If you have the date of an event from a reliable index it is relatively easy to ask to have a copy of the entry sent to you by a library or archive. They might expect payment in advance and ask you to sign a copyright form.

County Record Office and the Diocesan Record Office are separate (one in Stafford and the other in Lichfield) a phone call pays a double dividend – making absolutely certain that you are heading for the right place.

Local libraries and history centres might have microfilm copies or printed transcripts of parish registers for their area and the library of the Society of Genealogists in London has an excellent collection of both. The Society's publication *The National Index of Parish Registers* gives guidance on the whereabouts of original registers, with a volume for each county or for a group of counties. The Family History Centres of the Church of Jesus Christ of Latter-day Saints (LDS) can, for a small fee, order a copy of a parish register or bishops' transcript from their vast library in Utah. Members of the LDS church, or Mormons as we usually know them, regard tracing their family's history as an integral part of their faith and they are happy to share their facilities with everyone. Not all parish registers are available for ordering in this way but they have an extensive collection. They are likely, in any case, to have some copies of registers for their local area readily available. The centres are usually free to use but there are small fees charged for copying, printing and ordering microfilm on loan from the LDS library.

Later registers might still be in the hands of the individual church. If that is the case, try sending a letter to the incumbent to find out if they are willing to let you visit to search for an entry, or if they can copy the entry for you. (Always enclose a stamped, self-addressed envelope.) Given the difficult state of the finances of most churches it is reasonable to expect to pay a fee or make a donation for this. Please be understanding if it takes time – family history enquiries are unlikely to be high on the list of priorities of the average hardworking parish priest. If the parish does not have its own incumbent you should find contact details from the website A Church Near You.

Electronic images of some parish registers are already appearing online and more are likely in the future, so keep an eye open for developments in the county and local archives that interest you. Some, like the London Metropolitan Archives on Ancestry, will be the result of deals between archives and family history websites. Others will be due to the efforts of the archives themselves to digitalize and make available their own holdings, and of Family History Societies who have produced registers on CD for churches in their area. The LDS church is also making moves to put online its own vast collection of genealogical material.

Archives in Wales

In many ways the organization of archives in Wales echoes that in England. However, the National Library of Wales in Aberystwyth probably assumes a greater importance in that it might hold original or microfilm parish and nonconformist records that one would also expect to find in a county archive. The National Library of Wales is a good first port of call for pre-1837 research in Wales particularly if you believe your family might be spread over more than one county.

The National Library of Wales has a very helpful website. They also recommend C. J. Williams and J. Watts-Williams *Cofrestri Plwyf Cymru/Parish Registers of Wales* for details of deposited registers and the *National Index of Parish Registers* (Society of Genealogists).

THE ANGLICAN CHURCH IN WALES
Many of us think of Wales as having always been essentially nonconformist in its worship but this was far from being the case. Nonconformity did not take much of a hold in Wales until the late-eighteenth century and the same things that continued to tie people to the parish in England tied them to the parish in Wales – a need for parish assistance, for a place of burial and the need to

marry. As in England, therefore, the Anglican Church in Wales registers are an essential part of the search for Welsh ancestry.

Parish registers for Wales can be found either at the National Library of Wales or at the county record office for the county in which the parish lies. As in England, a few might still be in the parish itself. A small parish might still be struggling to fill a register issued in the nineteenth century. According to John Watts-Williams, writing in *Welsh Family History: A Guide to Research*, parish registers in Wales have a poorer survival rate than those in England. Only one parish register in Wales – Gwaunysgor in Flintshire – dates back to 1538 but survival in Wales is thought to be better than that in Scotland, Ireland and some other European countries. You should encounter little difficulty with language in Welsh parish registers since they were subject to the same rules as those in England. The Welsh language was not permitted to be used, although it will appear in the form of names. However, you are likely to encounter difficulties doing research using parish registers in Wales because fewer registers have survived. Welsh researchers are therefore more likely to be dependant upon Parish Chest documents (*see* Chapter 8). See also John Rowlands in *Welsh Family History: A Guide to Research.*

FLEET MARRIAGES
Fleet Marriages, also called irregular marriages, were conducted mainly in the vicinity of the Fleet Prison in London between 1667 and 1753 when Hardwicke's Marriage Act put paid to them by regulating marriage more heavily. These marriages were conducted by Church of England clergyman in accordance with the rites of the church but usually in the absence of banns or licence. At the time it was a popular way of getting married. According to the National Archives, who hold most of the records, up to about fifteen per cent of all marriages in England during the 1740s were Fleet Marriages. They attracted people who wanted to marry with minimum fuss. While it is undoubtedly true that the lack of questioning of both parties would attract a few rogues, relatively recent research shows that a lot of the marriages were as ordinary as those taking place in parish churches around the country.

Why do I need to find them?

If you have tried and failed to find a marriage, particularly if your ancestors lived in the London area, the Fleet marriage registers provide another chance of locating the ceremony. If you are lucky enough to find a Fleet marriage entry there is likely to be more detail than in ordinary Parish Registers of the time. It is possible that you will find an occupation given for the groom and details of where both parties came from. Some of the marriages were performed outside the prison including in the surrounding area, also known as 'the Rules', and in the Mayfair Chapel.

How do I find them?

Most records of Fleet marriages were in the hands of the individual clergymen who performed them and many have been lost. Most of those that survived until 1821 are now held at the National Archives at Kew, London in series RG7. There is also one register at the Bodleian Library in Oxford. Estimates vary of the exact number of marriages for which records survive but the National Archives puts it at over 200,000. There are indexes included in some of the volumes but your best hope of finding someone is to consult the increasing number of indexes to Fleet marriages being prepared by members of Family History Societies and others. Hertfordshire Family History Society has indexed 6,500 names of Hertfordshire people who married in this way (a useful note to their introduction advises that if you find an entry look to see if there is also a notebook, which might contain more information). There is also an index of Fleet registers whose brides and grooms came from Kent, Sussex and Surrey, and the Friends of Westminster Archives have identified three thousand possible Fleet marriages mentioned in the settlement examinations for St Martin in the Fields. Copies of all these are at the National Archives. Some Fleet marriages have found their way into the International Genealogical Index. The Genealogist website also offers an index to some of the Fleet marriage records in series RG7 at the National Archives.

OTHER IRREGULAR MARRIAGES

People did not necessarily have to travel to London to tie the knot in an 'irregular' fashion. There were parishes around the country, in both England and Wales, where the incumbent was known not to ask too many questions. These will be identifiable through local history books or possibly by looking at the marriage registers and finding a high proportion of marriages compared to the size of the population.

INDEXES TO PARISH REGISTERS

Indexes, where they exist, are a great help and can save you many hours searching page by page through parish and other registers. However, they are not a substitute for a register – just a way of getting to the right one more quickly. Not all parish registers have been indexed, and not all indexes are online.

THE INTERNATIONAL GENEALOGICAL INDEX (IGI)

The IGI is probably the best known of the major free indexes. It has long been the first port of call for researchers looking for a baptism or marriage of their ancestors. It contains very few burials. Available online at the Familysearch website, two versions of it are also commonly available on microfiche – 1988 and a revised version published on microfiche again in 1992. These versions are often held by libraries and archives. It is also available on the computers at Family History Centres run by the Church of Jesus Christ of Latter-day Saints.

The IGI was compiled by members of the Church of Jesus Christ of Latter-day Saints (also known as Mormons) to help their own church members compile their family trees. They do this as a part of their religious practice. It is, however, open to the general public to use in their own research. Copies of the IGI are available online, in public libraries and archives or in the LDS Family History Centres scattered around the world and usually attached to Mormon churches. LDS Family History Centres welcome people, of all faiths and none, who are doing their family history research. Opening hours and availability of facilities can be limited so it is better to book in advance. You can find the address of the one nearest to you at the Familysearch website.

Using the International Genealogical Index

The different versions of the IGI are not identical either in form or content, so if you are stuck and get the chance to see all versions it might help you in your search. A lot of the same names and events are in each version of the IGI but some are not. For example, when the 1988 version was re-issued as the 1992 version quite a large number of names were missed out so if you cannot find someone online or in 1992 try searching out a 1988 microfiche version for the county you are interested in. There might be one at your local library or archives, or at the library of the Society of Genealogists.

The microfiche versions of the IGI were issued county by county so some local libraries and archives might only hold the IGI for their own county and the surrounding areas but many will offer internet access to the online version.

Most people nowadays consult the IGI online at the Familysearch website. This has taken the work further with more names and events added. You can elect to search the IGI only or in conjunction with other databases. Read the search guidance carefully first because if you put in too much or too little information you will not get the best out of your search.

The IGI has its own individual way of indexing. It groups together not only names that are spelled similarly – like Gutteridge and Gutheridge – but also those that might sound the same – like Gudridge or Goodridge. This can be very helpful but it is also a good idea to think about how you would tackle an index without this help and check if any variants on the spelling you might otherwise have looked for are also there. The IGI for Wales has its own traits which are very clearly explained by Chris Pitt Lewis in *Welsh Family History: A Guide to Research* (ed. Rowlands).

The names in the microfiche IGI are listed alphabetically by surname including the variants, then by forename alphabetically in year order. An online search enables you to specify an area and a time period for your search.

In all versions of the IGI there are two main types of information available: that which has been copied or 'extracted' from a church register or bishop's transcript and that which has been submitted by a church member. Generally speaking the extracted information is held to be more reliable than the submitted information much of which is very helpful but some of which is little more than wishful thinking. The online version of the IGI identifies each type clearly at the foot of each individual entry.

When running your eyes down the list of names online, be wary of entries that start with the word 'about' and a date because these are most likely to be the result of a guess on someone's part. Look to see if there is any note as to exactly where the information has come from and if there is any background available. You can follow it up through the references given, but some of the entries are old. If using the microfiche version look at the column headed 'Batch No'. If the entry has been extracted its reference usually starts with a letter such as C, M or P. The references for information submitted by members usually just contain numbers.

In any event, whichever type of entry takes your interest, you should always check the original entry in the church register.

Which registers are included in the International Genealogical Index?

That is probably a more difficult question than you would think. It is important, again, to note that many registers do not appear in the IGI and information from those registers that do appear will not necessarily cover the dates you are looking for.

For the microfiche version look at the Parish and Vital Records List, published on microfiche in 1994. This tells you which parishes might be covered and for what dates. For administrative reasons it might not be wholly accurate but it is definitely a help.

For the online version consult the independent website compiled by Hugh Wallis at the Freepages website. From millions of names available on the IGI he has compiled a list of parishes and periods covered. He makes no claims for complete accuracy but it is a great help and an amazing piece of work. There is a link from the site direct to FamilySearch which enables you to find an individual parish register in the Batch Numbers site and then type in your family name to extract the examples in a particular register.

As always, follow up any findings in the IGI with a look at the original register. In the process, use your head. Your ancestors might appear to have moved parish but how do you know they are yours? What if the indexed entry does not fit in with what you already know? You need, then, to do a lot of further research to prove that the people you have found are your family members. Looking at neighbouring parishes that might not be included in the index should be high on your list, in case your family are hidden from view in a parish that is not indexed.

The British Isles Vital Records Index

This was compiled on CD by the Church of Jesus Christ of Latter-day Saints as an additional source to the IGI. Many libraries and archives have a copy, including the library at the Society of Genealogists, and it should be available at LDS Family History Centres as well. Few of the baptisms and marriages in this index are also in the IGI. However, like the IGI, its coverage by parish and year is not exactly certain but, in addition to parish register entries, it is known to include some entries from the Protestant Dissenters' Registry and the Wesleyan Methodist Registry (*see* Chapter 7).

Pallot's Marriage Index

This index covers marriages 1780–1837 mostly in Middlesex and London, including most of the parishes in the City of London but there are also some from a number of counties outside the South East. It is now available online at the Ancestry website and on CD. The Institute of Heraldic and Genealogical Studies in Canterbury holds the original.

Pallot's Baptism Index

This contains baptism entries from London and Middlesex 1780–1837 and it is available online at the Ancestry website and on CD. The Institute of Heraldic and Genealogical Studies in Canterbury holds the original. Part of the index was destroyed during World War II but there are still over a hundred thousand entries.

Boyd's Marriage Index

This is an index to marriages in England between 1538 and 1840. All counties are represented but some have much better coverage than others. A lot depended on what was available to Percival Boyd and others when they were compiling the index. It is available online at the Origins Network website and the original is held by the Society of Genealogists. It contains more than seven million names from well over four thousand parishes. London and Middlesex are heavily represented.

Most entries contain names of both bride and groom, the date, parish and county where the marriage took place. They also tell you where the information has come from. It is estimated that approximately fifteen per cent of the marriages during the period are represented, making it the largest single index to marriages before 1837. Under the heading Parish Details by County you can find which parishes are covered and for which dates. There is also a Society of Genealogists' publication *A List of Parishes in Boyd's Marriage Index* giving similar information.

Origins Network have added a supplement to the index, compiled by Cliff Webb, containing approaching another hundred thousand marriages in London and Middlesex, including over three thousand Jewish and the same number of Roman Catholic marriages. Work is ongoing to add more to the database. Consult the breakdown available with the supplement details to see if a parish you are interested in is included.

Boyd's London Burials

This index contains nearly a quarter of a million burials of adult males in the London area between 1538 and 1872. It has been supplemented on Origins Network by Cliff Webb's City of London Burials index and the St Leonard Shoreditch Burials 1813–1853 compiled by the Society of Genealogists. A detailed breakdown of contents and coverage of each index is available at the Origins website.

Searching for a burial in the London area has long been a thankless task, as it is in many cities. The close proximity and number of churches in the City of London in particular makes these burial indexes particularly useful.

Margareta ROGERS d/o Thomae	bap 5 June
Willielmus WILSON s/o Richardi	bap 7 June
Predictus Willielmus WILSON	bur 15 June
Willielmus FOUDEN and Anna FRAUNCIS	mar 21 June
Maria NICHOLSON d/o Willielmi	bap 29 June
Joannes HANSON and Brigita RIDGELEY	mar 7 July
Joannes BYCKER s/o Robarti born and	bur 9 July
Margareta MORRES d/o Willielmi	bap 17 July
Constancia d/o Willielmi JESPER and Jhouna STARTEN	bap 22 July

This Yeare 1584 the fyfth daye of August was the house at the Trent Yeat Buylded, or as we saye begonne to be reared, which house was Buylded by Henry GRYFFETH, Esquire, and the same yeare at the feast of the Nativitie of St John Baptiste before was the same Henry GRYFFETH made one of the Justices of the Peace within the County of Stafford.

Constancia JESPER d/o Willielmi	bur 6 August
Robartus RENOLD	bur 12 August
Fraunciscus DARRINGTON s/o Radulphi born and	bur 13 August
Agneta FOWDEN d/o Thomae	bap 12 September
Henricus MARSHALL and Elena COWPER	mar 13 September
Georgeus SCOFFILD s/o Thomae	bap 19 September
Susanna MILNER d/o Walteri	bap 26 September
Georgeus SCOFFILD s/o Thomae	bur 16 November
Jhouna BURWEY d/o Walteri	bap 19 November
Joannes MARSHALL s/o Nicolaii	bap 19 November
Willielmus FINNEY s/o Edmundi	bap 28 November
Agneta FOWDEN d/o Thomae	bur 13 December
Anna JESPER d/o Willielmi	bap 20 December
Page 27	
Anna WOODE d/o Joannis	bap 31 January
Elizabetha SHAWE, Vidua	bur 4 February
Henricus DANIELL and Elena HANSON	mar 4 February
Elena MOGE d/o Joannis	bap 5 February
Katherina MINORS d/o Houmfridi of Blacknole	bur 6 February
Maria GILBERT d/o Joannis	bur 11 February
Jhonna HOMES, Vidua	bur 22 February
Jhouna ELIOTE d/o Jacobi born and	bur 27 February
Agneta FUSDALE d/o Thomae	bur 3 March
Richardus HEATHCOTE als WILNER	bur 10 March
Willielmus GRESLEY s/o Edwardi	bur 13 March
Rogerus BELCHER, servus vicarii	bur March [n.d]

ANO DNI 1585 REG RE ELIZABETH 27	
Willielmus MEO s/o Joannis	bap 29 March
Brigitta WALKER d/o Walteri	bap 4 April
Jhonna MOUMFORT d/o Thomae born and	bur 19 April
Jhouna MOUMFORT wife of Thomae	bur 28 April
Anna SMITH als BALL d/o Johis SMITH	bap 1 May
Maria PARKER, Vidua	bur 7 May

A page from a printed transcript of an early register. Staffordshire Parish Registers Society. ALREWAS Parish Registers. Part 1 1547–1670 pub 2003. (Reproduced with the kind permission of the SPRS.)

Latin in Parish Registers

There are some very useful books on Latin for family historians. Most reference libraries and archives will have one on their shelves. Many names will be recognizable but some might cause you difficulty.

Some of the most common names

Carolus	Charles
Guillelmus	William
Jacobus	James
Johannes	John
Ricardus	Richard
Xpofer	Christopher

(This last is an abbreviation. Think of Christmas and Xmas.)

Commonly used words

Baptizatus	baptised
Dies	day
Filia	daughter
Filius	son
Generosa	lady, gentlewoman
Generosus	gentleman
Matrimonium	marriage
Natus	born
Nuptus	married
Sepultat	buried
Uxor	wife
Vidua	widow

The endings of some words will change according to tense and gender. If you come across something you don't understand, copy it down exactly as written so you can look it up later or ask a member of staff at the archives where you are looking at the documents. See also *A Latin Glossary for Family and Local Historians* by Janet Morris. More names, and Roman Numerals, appear in *The Local Historian's Encyclopedia* by John Richardson. A useful tip with numerals: a number such as eight – viii – is often written with a letter j as the last digit (as in viij). You can get a 'translation' by typing 'Roman Numerals' into an internet search engine, or in John Richardson's *The Local Historian's Encyclopedia*.

The National Burials Index

This has been compiled by the Federation of Family History Societies (FFHS) by amalgamating work done by member societies around the country. It is available on CD from the FFHS and also online at Findmypast. There is a breakdown on the CD of what parishes are covered and for which dates. Some of the entries had not been checked when the CD was produced, and these are noted as well. The online version is part of a co-operative effort between the website and the Federation of Family History Societies to publish digitally the information in some of the indexes produced by member societies. This includes indexes to baptisms and marriages as well as burials (*see* Chapter 11 for Monumental Inscriptions).

Other indexes to Parish Registers

The major online providers of sources for family history, having mostly completed their publication of census returns, have turned their focus to producing indexes to parish registers in co-operation with family history societies and other groups. The list of what is being provided online changes almost daily so it is a good idea to do a check of their new releases from time to time or subscribe to their mailing lists to get information about what they have produced.

Family history magazines are another good source of information about what is new online, and the website GENUKI generally keeps abreast of what is available for each county although the level of information varies depending on who is looking after each county's input.

If an index is not available online it can be difficult to track down. The Society of Genealogists holds a copy of a very large number of them so its library catalogue, online at the website, can be a good place to start to see if one is in existence for the parish in which you have an interest. County archives have often been presented with copies for their own county. Some are in the hands of individuals who might advertise the fact but many of these independent indexes seem to be finding their way online through the companies mentioned above. If you do not have access to the internet at home you can book a session at many libraries and archives and someone will always be glad to help you if you are not experienced in searching.

Printed Transcripts of Parish Registers

Long before the computer age many counties had their own Parish Register Societies dedicated to transcribing and publishing transcripts, some including indexes, of the parish registers in their county. They continue their work today. You can find these printed versions on the shelves of public libraries and archives and they are still as valuable a finding aid as they were when they were first produced.

Before you attempt to read a parish register in a library or county archive, particularly an early register, look around you to see if on the shelf there is a printed copy of it, or one on CD. If there is, it can be a great help in finding the entries you are looking for. Early registers can be a bit difficult to read and it is a great help to find that someone who knew what they were doing has got there before you. The transcription in these copies is usually of a very high standard.

If the register you are looking at is written in Latin the transcript can be doubly helpful, particularly if you are unfamiliar with both the language and the handwriting in the register (see page 85).

A lot of these transcripts have been used in compiling the indexes now available online. Some, particularly those produced by the long-established publisher Phillimore, have been reproduced on CD and are available at online retailers such as S & N Genealogy Supplies. Others are available either in printed or electronic form from individual Parish Register Societies.

When you have found your entry in the printed copy – check it with the original. The people who did the transcribing would be the first to tell you to do this, however much confidence they had in their work.

BISHOPS' TRANSCRIPTS

What are Bishops' Transcripts?

Before 1837 the nearest England and Wales came to any kind of centralized system of recording of life's major events was the annual compilation of Bishops' Transcripts (known as BTs) of entries in their own registers by incumbents of the Church of England. The transcripts date from 1598 but not all have survived. They were sent to the diocese and are still to be found in Church of England diocesan and/or county archives in England. Welsh BTs from 1661 can be found at the National Library of Wales. If you have found a parish register entry and there is a BT for the same period it is always worth looking at both in case more information is contained in one than the other. Likewise, if you have not found a parish register entry for your ancestor there is always an outside chance that the event was recorded in the BT without being recorded in the register. Leave no page unturned.

This is particularly true of research in Yorkshire up to 1812 where some additional information may have found its way into the Bishops' Transcripts in the 1770s, with the introduction of the Dade Registers, instead of being written in the parish registers (*The Goldmine of Dade Registers* by Kathryn Senior, Pontefract Family History Society 2003, www.pontefractfhs.org.uk).

HIGHFIELD ST JAMES
UNITED REFORMED CHURCH
HUDDERSFIELD

Highfield St James United Reformed Church, Huddersfield, Yorkshire (now Waverley United Reformed Church) by Hilary Berry. (Reproduced by kind permission of the artist.)

7 Nonconformist, Catholic and Jewish Registers

NONCONFORMISTS

What is a nonconformist?

The society our ancestors lived in was dominated to a massive degree by the Church of England; its ceremonies, rules and expectations. From Tudor times the Church of England baptized, married and buried the population. It granted probate to their wills (*see* Chapter 5). Its courts oversaw their behaviour. It was largely responsible for financial help to individuals in times of hardship.

Religious nonconformists, also known as 'dissenters' chose not to conform to the practices of the Church of England. Some disagreed slightly with its rules, others more so. There was no single 'Nonconformist Church'. Instead there were several different groupings of people who grew away from the Church of England to varying degrees.

The best-known nonconformists were the Quakers, Baptists, Presbyterians (also known as Unitarians), Congregationalists (also known as Independents) and Methodists. For many, embracing an alternative faith was a matter of belief and principle. Others perhaps found it convenient to attend the nonconformist chapel on the street where they lived rather than walk up the road to the Church of England (one very good reason to include maps in your search). Or they might have attended the nonconformist chapel in which their employer had a particular interest.

Patrick Palgrave-Moore's *Understanding the History and Records of Nonconformity* gives a good account of the growth of Puritanism (those who wanted to 'purify' all traces of Catholicism from the practices of the Church of England) and the emergence of early nonconformist groups. He gives the early 1640s as the date of the earliest surviving records of nonconformist baptism, but most surviving registers date from much later.

Nonconformist registers – Why do I need them?

Nonconformist registers, when they have survived, can give more information about a person than an equivalent entry in the registers of the Church of England. For that reason they are well worth the effort involved in pursuing them. In the early days, in particular, the entries might be included in Church Books, which also recorded details of the day-to-day running of the church.

In general, nonconformist registers of birth or baptism have not survived in large numbers for the seventeenth century but more have survived from the eighteenth century onwards. Marriage and burial registers are fewer for reasons discussed below.

Nonconformity often appealed in particular to the growing middle classes, so if your ancestor was in trade or a so-called 'white collar' job it is possible that they might have embraced alternative forms of worship at some time in their life.

1837 to the present

You can find the births, marriages and deaths of nonconformists in the General Register Office indexes from 1837 to the present day (see Chapter 2).

Where can I find records mentioning nonconformists?

Some nonconformists kept their own registers but many did not. Of those registers that were maintained many have not survived. (Some details of how to find those that have survived are given below under the headings for the different branches of nonconformity.) However, even if your ancestors were nonconformists it is still possible that they will be found in the registers of the Church of England. Ironically, it might be that the first registers you check for the baptism, marriage or burial of many nonconformists are those of the Church of England.

One reason for this is that until the start of civil registration in 1837 brought the certificates of birth, marriage and death that are familiar to us today, an extract from a Register of Baptism of the Church of England was the chief way in which people proved their identity. Similarly, legal processes – in the Courts of Chancery for example – could demand other proofs such as that of marriage or burial. In these circumstances, too, the Church of England was the first port of call.

'Occasional conformity'

Proof of identity and the fact that a traceable background with the Church of England was essential to some careers are two reasons why you might find nonconformists in the registers of the Church of England. Many people, apart from the most dedicatedly religious nonconformists, would take part in the ceremonies of the Church of England while also attending the church or chapel of their conscience. What Breed calls an 'atmosphere of occasional conformity' (p3 of Geoffrey R. Breed *My Ancestors were Baptists*) prevailed. Yet another reason lies in some early-eighteenth century legislation meaning that any child born to a so-called 'dissenter' should be entered into the registers of the Church of England. This was not always done but you

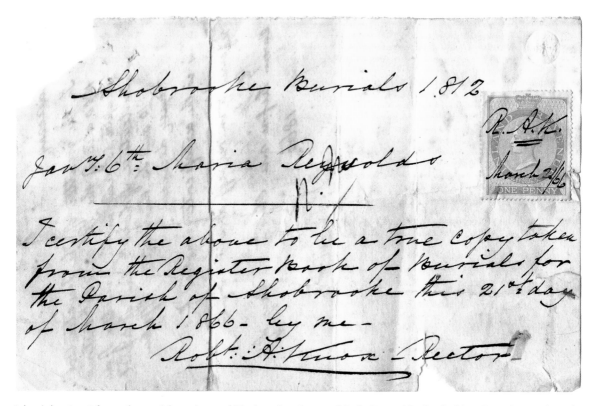

A burial extract from the parish register of Shobrooke, Devon. Maria Reynolds, buried in 1812. (Reproduced by kind permission of the Rector and Churchwardens of St Swithun's Shobrooke.)

might be lucky enough to find a 'birth' mentioned in the register without reference to a subsequent baptism or burial which would be a clue pointing towards it perhaps being a reported nonconformist birth.

It is highly unlikely that your nonconformist ancestors will be identified as nonconformists if they are mentioned in Anglican or Church of England parish registers. However, if you know they remained in the area and draw a blank looking there for other events in their lives, or if other clues arise to suggest non-conformity, that might be your cue to widen the search to take in any surviving nonconformist sources. One

possible clue is the example given by Anthony Camp who suggests that nonconformists marrying in the Church of England were more likely to be married by licence 'to avoid the indignity of having banns called on three successive Sundays' (p11 of Anthony Camp *My Ancestors Moved in England and Wales*).

NONCONFORMISTS IN WELSH PARISH REGISTERS

While today we associate Wales with nonconformity it did not really take hold until the late- eighteenth century, but then it grew very rapidly. According to John Watts-Williams, by 1837 'for every five recorded baptisms there is one...not recorded' (see *Welsh Family History: A Guide to Research* ed. Rowlands, pp21 and 22) in the parish registers of the Anglican Church in Wales. The rate for England was one in twenty-six. Then by 1851 'eight out of every ten Welsh men and women, who attended a place of worship, went to chapel rather than to church'.

NONCONFORMIST BURIALS

Many nonconformists were buried in Church of England burial grounds for practical reasons to do with public health and because they had nowhere else to be buried. It was, and is, the right of every parishioner to be buried in the parish churchyard, space permitting. The same applies to anyone dying within the parish. Some parish churches set aside a piece of ground for the purpose. Dedicated nonconformist burial grounds were gradually established but most date from as late as the nineteenth century. One of the few exceptions is Bunhill Fields in London, which had burials from 1665 to 1852. Surviving registers date from 1713. They are held at the National Archives in Kew, London. Ballast Hills Cemetery in Newcastle has registers from 1792 and Monumental Inscriptions dating from 1707. Some of these monu-mental inscriptions might be your only clue to a burial if the registers have not survived.

CENTRALIZED NONCONFORMIST REGISTERS BEFORE 1837

DR WILLIAMS'S LIBRARY

Nonconformists, also widely known as dissenters, were concerned about the failure of many of their

---

Nonconformist marriages and Hardwicke's Marriage Act

In 1753 Hardwicke's Marriage Act decreed that all marriages, in order to be deemed legal, should take place in parish churches, according to the rites of the Church of England. The Act had been passed to try to put an end to so-called 'irregular marriages'.

Of the nonconformists, only Quakers were exempted, but the others – Baptists, Methodists, Congregationalists among them – were affected by the Act. Therefore for that period you are highly likely to find your nonconformist marriage in the Church of England, also known as the Anglican Church. Jewish marriages were also exempt.

The same applied in Wales, where Quakers and Jews formed a smaller percentage of the population than in England. It is therefore probably even more likely that a marriage in Wales during the period 1754 to 1837 would be recorded in the registers of the Anglican Church in Wales.

From 1837, the beginning of civil registration, until 1898 marriages could be performed in nonconformist chapels with a civil registrar present, so you should be able to find marriage certificates by looking in the civil registration indexes for the period. After 1898 the presence of a registrar at the ceremony was no longer a requirement, but the registrar would get a copy from the register so you should still find nonconformist marriages registered in the civil registration system, using their centralized indexing system (see Chapter 2).

B. N° 933.   185 D

THESE are to Certify, That *Henry Smithers*
Son   of *Joseph Smithers*
and *Martha*   his Wife, who was Daughter of
John and Alice Keene was Born in *Crooked Lane*
                    in the Parish of *S.t Michael*
in the City of *London*   this *Seventh*
Day of *August*   in the Year *1762*
at whose Birth we were present. *Catharine Keene*

Regiſtred at Dr. *Williams's* Library, in *Redcroſs-ſtreet*, near *Cripplegate, London.*

June 10.. 1776. James Pickbourn Regiſter.

congregations to keep a proper record of births and baptisms. The Dissenting Deputies, representatives of the leading groups of Protestant nonconformists, established a central system of registration to record births. Those who used it were mainly Presbyterians, Congregationalists – also known as Independents – and Baptists, but other nonconformists used it too.

Although the register that they established dates from 1742, it records events as early as 1716 because people were allowed to register births that had occurred before the system was set up. While it was London based, it was used widely – even by parents abroad. The librarian at Dr Williams's Library was separately employed by the Dissenting Deputies to act as registrar and because of this the register became associated with the Library's name.

The idea of a central registry was so successful that the Wesleyan Methodists created their own in 1818 with some retrospective entries going back to 1773. If you are lucky enough to find the birth of an ancestor in these particular records you could find details of three generations.

When civil registration was introduced in 1837 these registries became redundant and now both sets of records are at the National Archives at Kew as part of the series RG4 and RG5. There are online indexes available to both series – chiefly through the BMD Registers website – and others are being developed but, as always, read the small print and check thoroughly exactly what is being offered and whether or not the information is complete. If in doubt keep going back to the sites and checking to see if more has been added. There is a charge for looking at the registers online, but you can see them free at the National Archives.

Dr Williams's Library itself is still in existence as the principal library for research into Protestant Dissent. It has a great deal on the history of religious dissent but little by way of genealogical information except for the records of London Unitarian congregations and the Old General Baptist congregations of London, Kent and Sussex.

INDIVIDUAL REGISTERS NOW HELD CENTRALLY

After civil registration of births, marriages and deaths was introduced in 1837 the registers of individual nonconformist churches, so-called 'non-parochial registers', and Catholic registers were required to be 'surrendered' to the Registrar General. Not all of them conformed to the request. Those registers that were surrendered during the following few years, and after a further request in 1858, are now held at the National Archives at Kew in London under series RG4 to RG8.

County and local archives

Many county and local archives hold microfilm copies of the surrendered registers for their area, along with some other local nonconformist registers that have been

---

Indexes

The BMD Registers website has an index to and images of a large number of those individual nonconformist registers held at the National Archives. There is a charge to see the images online but it is free if you visit the National Archives.

Many nonconformist records, but not those of Quakers, are included in the International Genealogical Index produced by the Church of Jesus Christ of Latter-day Saints (also known as the Mormons). Around eighty per cent of the birth entries in the Dr Williams's Library collection and the Wesleyan Methodist Registry are said to be on their British Vital Records Index CD, which is held by many libraries and archives, and at the Mormon Family History Centres around the country (see Chapter 12).

---

deposited with them since for safe-keeping. Check with them to see what they have.

EARLY REGISTERS OF INDIVIDUAL NONCONFORMIST DENOMINATIONS

BAPTISTS

The chief difference, for the purposes of genealogy, between Baptists and other nonconformists is that Baptists do not baptize infants. Any baptism records you find for members of the Baptist church are likely to be for adults. They did, however, often make a record of births.

The Baptists evolved in England from a group who came over from Holland in 1611 and in Wales the first Baptist church was founded in 1639. Unlike the Methodists and the Church of England there was no central organization – each church governed itself, run by the 'church meeting'.

Like other nonconformist groupings, there were various movements, each with a different emphasis, for example the New Connexion, Particular Baptists and Strict Baptists.

Where can I find the registers?

Many Baptist registers dated up to 1837, along with those of other nonconformists, were surrendered to the Registrar General. Those that were surrendered can be found at the National Archives at Kew. There are also likely to be copies at local and county archives. Some might still be with the Baptist churches themselves but the archives would be able to advise you whether this is likely.

For more information consult Geoffrey R. Breed's My Ancestors were Baptists.

(Don't forget that many early nonconformists can be found in the registers of the Church of England.)

CONGREGATIONALISTS AND INDEPENDENTS

Independents grew from dissent within the Church of England during the sixteenth century. Their beliefs largely echoed those of the Puritans and, like them, many were exiled. Their beliefs gained in popularity during and after the Civil War, and the Independents gained in social importance, but once the Monarchy was restored their star began to wane again. They became known as Congregationalists during the nineteenth century although some chapels retained the name Independent.

Like other nonconformist congregations many of their registers up to 1837 were deposited and are now at the National Archives at Kew. Others are held at county archives or are still with the individual congregations. For more information consult D.J.H. Clifford's *My Ancestors were Congregationalists in England and Wales.*

Many Congregational churches merged with the Presbyterians in 1972 to form the United Reformed Church. The website of the United Reformed Church Historical Society at (*see* website list) gives some guidance on the whereabouts of records and also on how best to make an approach direct to the congregation for information about your family history. (Don't forget that many early nonconformists can be found in the registers of the Church of England.)

METHODISTS

Methodism began, as an idea, in 1729 at Oxford University. In the early days it was a movement within the Church of England. They were known as Methodists because of their methodical approach to religion, with prayer meetings and daily readings. The two key players in the early days were John Wesley and George Whitefield. By 1741 they had disagreed over interpretation of the Gospels and the first of many splits in the movement occurred.

Wesley preached up and down the country and his followers, and those of Whitefield, built preaching houses to accommodate their meetings, in which some early baptisms took place. Most children, however, were still baptized in the Church of England. The Methodist movement remained within the Church of England until after Wesley's death in 1791, when the Wesleyan Methodist Church quickly emerged, but not as a whole entity. Several separate movements, all calling themselves Methodists, evolved. So when you are looking for records you will find Primitive Methodists, the Methodist New Connexion, the Countess of Huntingdon's Connection and other variations. Then these groupings began to join together to form other, larger, groupings finally resulting in what is now known as the Methodist Church formed in 1932. (*See* William Leary's *My*

Ancestors were Methodists and Richard Ratcliffe's *Basic Facts about Methodist Records for Family Historians.*)

Where can I find the records?

Not many Methodist records dated before 1800 survive. Methodist records, like those of other nonconformists, were called in by the Registrar General in 1837 and 1858 so copies of these registers can be found at the National Archives at Kew. Many local and county archives will have copies on microfilm of those deposited registers relating to their area.

Other individual Methodist registers are likely to be with county archives. Some will be 'circuit registers' because ministers looked after a number of congregations and tended to keep a personal register. When these have survived they are most likely to be in county archives. Others might still be with individual chapels.

Fortunately for family history researchers many early Methodist children were baptized in the Church of England but are unlikely to be identified as Methodists. A Wesleyan Methodist registry was established in 1818 to record Methodist baptisms.

There were some Methodist burial grounds for which records were kept. These are listed in Leary's *My Ancestors were Methodists* published by the Society of Genealogists and in county volumes of the *National Index of Parish Registers.* Individual county archives generally have lists of Methodist burial grounds. You will also find Methodists buried in Church of England parish burial grounds or civic burial grounds and cemeteries.

The John Rylands University Library in Manchester holds the Methodist Archives, and has established a Biographical Index, now available online. This comprises an online index to Methodist ministers and some lay people since the time of John Wesley. Over a thousand names of people mentioned in the letters and papers in the Methodist Archives are included.

PRESBYTERIANS AND UNITARIANS

The Presbyterians in England and Wales started as an early movement within the Church of England. Among other things they wanted to abolish some of the Church's rituals. The Scottish Presbyterians were a separate entity altogether, although they did found some of their own churches in England.

The Presbyterians gained in influence during the Civil War and, surviving a low point once the Monarchy was restored, went on to grow during the eighteenth and nineteenth centuries. Their doubts about the existence of the Holy Trinity led to them becoming known as Unitarians.

Like other nonconformists, some of their registers up to 1837 were deposited with the Registrar General and are now held at the National Archives at Kew. County and local archives are likely to have anything else that is not still with the individual congregations. Some of the church's journals date back to the eighteenth century and can include details of individuals. They are listed in Palgrave-Moore's *Understanding the History and Records of Nonconformity*. A. Ruston's *My Ancestors were English Presbyterians (Unitarians)* contains further information.

In 1972 the Presbyterians merged with the Congregationalists to form the United Reformed Church. The website of the United Reformed Church Historical Society gives some guidance on the whereabouts of records. They also advise on how best to make an approach direct to the congregation for information about your family history if you don't find what you are looking for at the archives.

RECORDS OF THE SOCIETY OF FRIENDS (QUAKER RECORDS)

The earliest Quaker meetings were held in the East Midlands of England during the late 1640s and early 1650s. The earliest records date from then, with a handful of retrospective entries.

Why do I need them?

The Society of Friends, often known as Quakers, kept itself apart from other religions. This distancing can partly be ascribed to the fact that, in the early years, Quakers suffered persecution for their beliefs (recorded in their Books of Sufferings). Their beliefs usually prevented them from participating, as many other nonconformists occasionally did, in Church of England rites and ceremonies – indeed they could be reprimanded for doing so. A search for Quaker ancestors in the registers of the Church of England is, therefore, likely to produce few results.

The Society of Friends has a reputation for meticulously kept records. They can be quite detailed in comparison with early Church of England records. These records were kept by the members themselves because there is no priesthood or ministry for the Society of Friends. Their worship traditionally takes the form of silent meetings, the silence only broken when a member feels moved to speak.

Quakers recorded births, not baptisms and, along with the Jews, were exempted from the necessity to marry in the parish church between 1754 and 1837. The Friends would not swear oaths or pay tithes to the Church of England. This latter, in particular, means that you might also find them in Quarter Sessions records (held at county archives) charged with non-payment.

Burial entries in the Friends' own registers can often also include a date of death. From very early on, they had their own burial grounds because they would not be buried in consecrated parish burial grounds. Survival of headstones is patchy owing to the fact that some regarded such things as personal vanity (for the same reason they also disliked painted portraits). Milligan and Thomas in *My Ancestors were Quakers* advise that there are occasional early entries in Church of England registers for burials of Quakers. The incumbent of the parish they lived in sometimes felt obliged, in accordance with the law, to record each burial in woollen in his parish, or each birth, even if the family did not worship at his church. (For more about burial in woollen, *see* Chapter 6.)

The Quakers had their own system of poor relief and would also write letters of introduction for Members moving to a new area, and therefore a new Meeting, so their records can be invaluable if your ancestors moved. They were, and still are, great believers in the value of education and founded several well-known schools, for which records might still be either with the school or the county archive.

DATES

The Friends started keeping registers from the early 1650s. Some guides to those registers give earlier dates, back into the late 1500s. This is because a few of their registers contain dates of birth entered retrospectively.

Quakers would not use the names of days or months associated with pagan deities, for example March, named after Mars, the Roman god of War. Instead they used numbers – the fourth day of the first month, for example. This was complicated by the change of calendar from the Old Style (Julian) calendar to the New Style (Gregorian) calendar in 1751–2 (*see* Chapter 6). Milligan and Thomas have a very good explanation of how this affected the keeping of records in an Appendix to their book *My Ancestors were Quakers*.

Where can I find the records?

In common with other nonconformists, the Society of Friends in England and Wales was obliged to hand over its records to the Public Record Office in 1837 and 1858, and the majority of these original registers are held at the National Archives, Kew, in class RG6.

Before they handed the original records over to the Public Record Office, the Society of Friends produced two copies of Digests of the information in the records. One copy was retained by the Quarterly Meeting and can often be found in county archives in the locality where the Meetings took place. Check before visiting because not all of these have survived and some might have had restrictions placed on them. More recent records might still be in the hands of the Meeting and, again, access might be restricted.

Note that the Digests are not transcripts of the original and might contain less information, so if you are looking for all the details of a particular event, including marriage witnesses for example, the original records from which the Digests were made should also be consulted at Kew.

The second version of each Digest was for national use and is now likely to be in the Library of the Society of Friends at Friends House in London – so the chances of one of the copies having survived are quite good. Consult their website for further information along with the website of the Quaker Family History Society. The Digests held at Friends House have been photographed and are available on microfilm – there is a copy at the Society of Genealogists.

After 1837 National Digests of Quaker births, marriages and deaths were compiled and sent to the Yearly Meeting. These are held by the Library of the Society of Friends in London.

Different types of Meeting dealt with different matters. The Digests were made from records of the Quarterly Meetings. Conditions varied, but the Quarterly Meetings had usually received the information on births, marriages and deaths from the more localized Monthly Meeting, who in turn had received the information from an even more localized Preparative Meeting. A good plan of action might be to consult the Digest first if possible and then go to the Monthly or Quarterly Meeting records in search of more detail. A useful Appendix in Milligan and Thomas lists the Quarterly Meetings in existence in 1840–42.

Like many nonconformist records, Quaker registers were often, in the early days, in the hands of individuals and therefore may not have survived. However, if they found their way, even briefly, into the Friends' system there must be a reasonable chance of finding some information somewhere.

SMALLER RELIGIOUS MOVEMENTS

Other, much smaller, groups of nonconformists formed or arrived in the country over the centuries.

There is a Moravian Church Archive and Library in Muswell Hill, London and details are available at their website under 'Archive'. It holds some surviving documents of closed churches, mission records and administrative records. Otherwise the Moravians' records are likely to be with individual churches or at the National Archives in series RG4. The example shown is from the Register of Births and Baptisms of the Moravian Church at Haverfordwest in Wales. It is an example of the kind of information that can, with luck, be found in nonconformist registers. This one gives a date, place and even time, of birth, a date and place of baptism and even notes the death of one of the baptized children nearly thirty years later and the possible marriage and removal of another to Bristol.

Some Swedenborgian or New Jerusalemites registers are also held at the National Archives in series RG4. Other small religious movements are discussed in Volume 2 of the *National Index of Parish Registers* published by the Society of Genealogists and Phillimore, available in

Children Born & Baptized, Since this Congrn was settled, Augt. 13. 1763.

Name	Parents	Born, when & where	Bapt. when & where	By whom
Martha Howell. now Lewis, Rotwell Street, near Bristol. Dept. a member of Bristol Congrn. 1805.	Daughter of Philip & Mary Howell.	1763. Octob: 16. at 5. o Clock in ye Morning in Key-Street, St. Thomas parish. Haverfordwest.	1763. Octob: 16. in the Brethrens-Hall, on the Key. Haverfordwest.	By Wr. Nyberg
William Jmanuel Sparks.	Son of John & Mary Sparks.	1763. Octob: 19. at 5. post meridiem, in Bridge-Street, St. Martins-parish. Haverfordwest.	1763. Octob: 23. in the Brethrens-Hall, on ye Key. Ditto.	By Wr. Nyberg
Jane Jones.	Daughter of James & Jane Jones.	1764. March 3. at 1 in the Morning, in Bridge-Street, St. Martins-parish. Haverfordwest.	1764. March. 4. in the Brethrens-Hall, on ye Key. Haverfordwest.	By Wr. Nyberg
James Lewis.	Son of Thos. & Eliz. Lewis.	1764. July 9. at 4. o Clock in ye afternoon, in Key-Street, St. Thomas-parish, Haverfordwest.	1764. July 12. in The Brethrens-Hall, on the Key. Do.	By Wr. Nyberg
John Bevan.	Son of Davd & Eliz. Bevan.	1764. Sept. 17. at 7. in the Morning, in St. Martins parish, Haverfordwest.	1764. Septr. 17. in The Breth: Hall on the Key. Haverfordwest.	By Wr. Nyberg
Mary Elizabeth Sparks. Dept. this life Jany 7, 1794, in her 29th year; was in our burying ground on the 12th	Daughter of John & Mary Sparks.	1765. Sept. 14. at 6. post meridiem, in Bridge-Street, St. Martins parish, Haverfordwest.	1765. Septr. 15. in The Brethrens-Hall on the Quay, Haverfordwest.	By Br. Nyberg
Nathanaël Deodatus Nyberg	Son of Lawr: Ths. & Martha Nyberg	1766. January 3. at 3 o Clock post merid. In the Congregation-House, on St. Thomas Green, St. Ths: parish. Haverfordwest.	1766. January 5. in The Brethrens Chapel on St. Thomas's Green. Being the first Bapz. d there.	By Br. Nyberg

A page from the Register of Births and Baptisms at the Moravian Church, Haverfordwest 1763. (Courtesy The National Archives ref RG4/4076 and by kind permission of the Moravian Church in Great Britain and Ireland.)

libraries and at the library of the Society of Genealogists. County volumes of the *NIPR* also list known instances of small religious movements in their county and state if registers are known to have survived.

The French Protestant Huguenots, according to Palgrave-Moore, had been 'absorbed into the Anglican community by 1800' (p26). The Huguenot Society of Great Britain and Ireland has a website offering advice to people who believe they might have Huguenot ancestry.

A small number of German Lutheran churches were founded in London during the eighteenth century in particular. Some of their registers have found their way to the National Archives. And the baptism records of a Swiss church in Soho Square can also be found at the National Archives in series RG4 under 'Foreign Churches'.

Where do I go from here?

If you have discovered nonconformists among your ancestors the obvious first step is to search further among the records to see if this was a 'one-off' occurrence or part of a family-wide pattern. Get to know the history of the religion's establishment in the area and if you do not find any further evidence at that particular place of worship try other places of worship belonging to the same branch of nonconformity. The *Victoria County History Series* can be very useful for this, and so can the Society of Genealogists' series the *National Index of Parish Registers*, which gives a breakdown at the beginning of each volume of various religions' relationship with each county, and goes on to list surviving registers.

Armed with that information, try to establish what other records, such as church minutes and magazines, have survived by making enquiries at the archives for the county and also more locally with the nearest library branch to where they lived. Do not forget that some nonconformist registers were deposited in 1837 and 1858 and are now in the National Archives, although many local archives now have microfilm copies of the deposited registers relating to their area.

Some registers might still be with the place of worship in question. In that case the best thing is to write a letter enquiring what their policy is in the case of family history enquiries and enclose a stamped, self-addressed envelope. You are more likely to get a positive response if your enquiry relates to a specific entry but expect possible delays in replying. Remember that family history enquiries are probably not going to be high on their list of priorities.

Check local directories in case the family was in business, and if you can establish that they moved look at a map to see if another more convenient place of worship grew up near to their new home. While nonconformists sometimes travelled many miles to attend a particular place of worship and hear a particular preacher, others would involve themselves locally. And don't forget the Church of England. With the usual exception of the Quakers, as discussed above, many nonconformists still had a relationship with the established Church. The certificates of birth, marriage and death issued by the General Register Office from 1837 will include nonconformists along with the rest of the population.

SEARCHING FOR JEWISH ANCESTORS

There is a long history of Jewish migration to this country. Having been expelled in the thirteenth century, Jewish immigrants started to return in secret in the reign of Elizabeth I. Portugal, Spain, Holland, Germany and Italy were the chief sources during the sixteenth and seventeenth centuries. Later centuries saw Jews fleeing persecution in Eastern Europe and then from Germany in particular up to and during the Second World War.

In many ways the same rules apply to researching a Jewish family as to any other family in England and Wales, particularly in the nineteenth, twentieth and twenty-first centuries. Jewish families made use of civil registration and would be found in trades directories and census returns. Here, the place of origin is of particular interest to you and, more than ever, it is important to find family members in as many censuses as possible (*see* Chapter 4). If your ancestors came here during the late-nineteenth century or early twentieth century there is a chance of discovering at least their country of origin from a census return. Occasionally the enumerator will have exceeded his duty and entered the name of a town or village, which is the equivalent of genealogical gold. A few ships' passenger lists might also be useful in this respect but look out for a change of name on arrival perhaps to a more anglicized version.

If the immigration predates the census years (national survival of census documents is from 1841 onwards) you might be dependent upon finding in census returns other family members who came over later from the same area. If a person was described in the census as a British Subject it is possible they had gone through the process of naturalization. Surviving papers for this process are in the National Archives at Kew, who have produced a very useful Research Guide which is available at their website.

BEFORE 1837

Before civil registration started in 1837, things get a little more difficult. Obviously there will be no records of baptism but it has been found that a few Jews, particularly in London, paid for the date of birth of their children to be entered in Church of England Parish Registers. This was to give them some proof of identity and citizenship. Extracts from Church of England registers were used for this purpose by the population in general when such proof was required. The entry itself might even identify the family as Jewish.

Hardwicke's Marriage Act excluded Jewish marriages from its provisions and, while Catholics and most nonconformists were obliged to marry in the Church of England between 1754 and 1837, Jews could conduct their own marriage ceremonies. There might be no marriage entry in a register but synagogues kept a copy of the marriage contract. Jewish registers were not surrendered to the Registrar General in 1837. In general they remain with the synagogues. After 1837 Jewish marriages would be picked up by the civil registration system and should be found in the General Register Office indexes.

Records of circumcision were not usually kept by the synagogues but a few may have survived in other hands. Bar Mitzvahs might have been announced in the newspapers, and the same might apply to marriages and deaths. *The Jewish Chronicle* started in 1841 and there were other, more localized, publications as well. Wealthy Jewish marriages might be found mentioned in *Gentleman's Magazine,* which dates from 1731 to the early-twentieth century. Monumental inscriptions in Jewish Burial Grounds can give dates and places of birth.

The Society of Genealogists has a large collection of Jewish genealogical papers and a copy of the *National Index of Parish Registers vol.3,* which describes some sources for Jewish Genealogy. The Jewish Genealogical Society of Great Britain has a very informative website. Membership gives access to a great many finding-aids and advice on the present whereabouts of records.

There is a lot of information and help available. Arm yourself with a guide such as the Society of Genealogists' *My Ancestors were Jewish* by Dr Anthony Joseph or the JGSGB's *A Guide to Jewish Genealogy in the United Kingdom* ed. Rosemary Wenzerul (JGSGB also advertise guides to research in Poland and other European countries) and make a start!

CATHOLIC ANCESTORS

Until Tudor times the people of England and Wales worshipped in churches that were Catholic, ruled from Rome. The establishment of the Church of England under Henry VIII led to some difficult times for Roman Catholics. They were fiercely persecuted, including long periods when the keeping of registers of any kind might be regarded as suicidal. Survival, therefore, of Roman Catholic registers is patchy and there is no single place where they can all be found. During the periods when Catholics were being actively persecuted, and up to at least the latter part of the nineteenth century, the Church operated as a series of missions. This meant that many of the registers were held in the personal possession of priests who moved around their area. In the early days the registers might just have been notes on pieces of paper that could easily be disposed of if necessary.

Catholicism remained strongest in the Midlands and the North of England. It was often the noble families who maintained the old faith. This meant that there were small pockets, whole villages often, where Catholicism survived under the protection of these noble families. Their servants, estate workers and the local yeomen were highly likely also to be Catholic. The estate papers of these families might yield some clues. These can be found at local archives or further afield if the family owned land in other parts of the country.

Catholics were debarred from the professions, from advancement in the army or from holding public office until the mid-nineteenth century. After the passing of

Recusant Rolls

The Church of England was, at some periods during its history, obliged to identify people who did not attend services. These people, many of them Catholics, but also Protestant nonconformists or dissenters, were known as recusants. Their names were recorded on documents called Recusant Rolls. Some copies of these still survive and can be found at the National Archives series E376 and E377. Other notes of fines imposed on Catholics and other recusants are also at the National Archives. Their research guide to Catholic Recusants is very helpful on this. It is also worth looking at locally held records, particularly the Churchwardens' Presentments and Quarter Sessions, who also dealt with recusants. Not much indexing has been done, so it might take a while.

Hardwicke's Marriage act in 1753 up to the introduction of civil registration in 1837 Catholics were among those supposed to marry in the Church of England. However, some were still married according to Catholic rites. From 1850 the Catholic Church regained its standing and there were Bishops and Dioceses once again. After that date their registers are much more likely to have survived.

WHAT CAN CATHOLIC REGISTERS TELL ME?

Baptism entries are most likely to have survived and should give the child's name, the parents' names (including the mother's maiden name) and the names of the child's sponsors. Lists of confirmations were made but often contain only basic information. Where marriage registers are available, there was no set format so the information can vary from very basic to very helpful.

Many Catholic churches kept no burial registers but deaths might be noted in a general register. Catholic burials can often be found in Church of England registers because there was, in the early days, nowhere else for them to go. The people buried there are unlikely to be identified as Catholic.

WHERE CAN I FIND THE REGISTERS?

Not many registers remain that date from before the early nineteenth century, and there is no single place to go to find them. The library at the Society of Genealogists may have copies of anything that has been produced in printed form or on microfiche and CD. Their online library catalogue would help you to see what is available. County and local archives are likely to have similar material relating to their own area, but always check before you go.

The Catholic National Library at Farnborough holds typewritten transcripts, indexes, printed transcripts of registers and CD copies, many deposited by the Catholic Family History Society. They do not have original registers. Access is free but a donation is appreciated. Contact them before visiting because they have limited opening hours and are heavily reliant on volunteers.

The Manchester and Lancashire Family History Society and the North West Branch of the Catholic Family History Society have transcribed and indexed some of the registers for their area in the Catholic Register Index. You can obtain details from either of their websites. The Catholic Family History Society holds other indexes including an index of about 14,000 nuns in English Orders giving date of birth and names of parents among other details. Other county societies, such as the Birmingham and Midland Society for Genealogy and Heraldry, the Staffordshire Parish Register Society and the Shropshire Parish Register Society, have produced transcripts of Catholic registers in their area. Libraries might also hold material published by the Catholic Record Society.

Original registers

Once you have found your ancestor in one of the transcripts you will want to check the details against the original register. A number of Catholic registers dated up to 1837, mainly from Yorkshire, Northumberland and Durham were deposited with the Public Record Office and will now be found at the National Archives at Kew in series RG4 and at BMD registers. The online registers can be seen for a fee or you can view them free by visiting the National Archives.

Michael Gandy's series of books *Catholic Missions and Registers 1700–1880* detailing the whereabouts of

Catholic registers is an excellent finding-aid. The Society of Genealogists' *National Index of Parish Registers* series Volume 3 includes 'Sources for Roman Catholic and Jewish Genealogy'. It is no longer in print but a copy is listed in the Society's library catalogue. Catholic churches also appear in county editions of the *NIPR*.

The Catholic Church's own Diocesan Archives vary in the number of original or microfilm copies of registers they hold, and in the amount of time they are able to give to dealing with members of the public. If in doubt about whom to contact, the county archive nearest to where your ancestors lived should be able to tell you which Catholic Diocese is relevant to your search. It would then be a good idea to write, enclosing a stamped self-addressed envelope, unless they give a contact telephone number. The same applies to enquiries made directly to a parish priest. Expect to have to pay a fee or make a donation. Addresses can be obtained from *The Catholic Directory*.

As always, do not expect an immediate reply. As Michael Gandy says in his introduction to *Catholic Missions and Registers 1700–1880* (p.xii) 'We really must be realistic and accept that priests really do have more important things to do than help us with our hobby.'

The Parish Chest was originally a place of safe-keeping in the Parish Church for the registers and other important parish records. (Photo Tom Ross.)

8 Records from the Parish Chest and Institutions

THE PARISH CHEST

Just because your ancestors were poor it does not mean that they left no clues to their existence other than entries in parish registers. You just have to work a bit harder to try and find them. The answer, if it is available, lies in documents kept by each parish in addition to the parish registers described in Chapter 6.

Many of the duties we now look to the State to fulfil were, for several centuries up to the nineteenth century, traditionally carried out by each parish. For example, before 1829 when policing gradually started to take on a different form thanks to Sir Robert Peel each parish (and before that, each manor) had appointed its own unpaid Constable. He performed a number of duties – from the removal of strangers and training the local militia to the care of the parish bull! Long before the Welfare State the poor looked to the parish for help when they were in difficulty and each parish appointed Overseers of the Poor to raise and administer the poor rate.

These responsibilities generated a number of written records. They were traditionally kept in a big wooden box in the church that also held the parish registers. So the documents themselves have become known as Parish Chest documents. If they have survived they are most likely to be in county archives.

Settlement

Poor Laws were passed with great regularity, and then amended, and then amended again and again, from Tudor times onwards until 1834, when the poor became the responsibility of the Poor Law Unions. During that period the parish took on more and more the task of regulating and caring for the poor in its midst. W.E. Tate's book *The Parish Chest* gives details of the various amendments over the years.

In order that the parish did not become overburdened with the cost of supporting people who did not belong there, one of the amendments to the Poor Law, in 1601, brought into focus the idea of settlement, of belonging to a particular parish whose responsibility you became in times of hardship. This meant that poor relief would only be paid by a parish to someone entitled to live there and receive relief. The rules about who was entitled to settle in a particular parish were simple at first but became more complicated with the Settlement Act of 1662 when stricter rules were laid down due to abuse of the system. Some of the qualifications leading to entitlement to poor relief were if a person:

- Had been born in the Parish.
- Had been employed in the Parish for more than 365 days.
- Held office in the Parish, for example Constable or Overseer of the Poor.
- Was apprenticed to a Master in the Parish.
- Having given public notice of arrival, had lived in the parish for more than forty days.
- Was married to a man of the parish (if the husband died this could lead to women from outside being separated from their wider family unless they were in a position to support her if she went home to them).

- A legitimate child under a certain age. (They would be settled in the parish of their father.)
- An illegitimate child born in the parish (this led, at one period, to pregnant women being transported over the parish boundary before they gave birth).
- Paying rent of a certain value per annum.

Adjustments were made to the laws and the rules of entitlement from time to time but it had the effect of restricting the free movement of labour. A side-effect was that the system has left documents that might give you some very useful information about your ancestors.

SETTLEMENT EXAMINATIONS, SETTLEMENT CERTIFICATES AND REMOVAL ORDERS

Why do I need them?

If documents relating to Settlement have survived for the parishes you are looking at, they can provide information that is very difficult to find anywhere else. From 1697, if an outsider came to a parish, they were expected to bring with them a certificate from their own parish, saying that they were chargeable to that parish if they fell on hard times. If such a certificate has survived, which is rare, it gives you valuable information about where your ancestor came from.

More likely to have survived is a record of an 'examination', or interview, usually by Justices of the Peace (generally local landowners or wealthier parishioners) questioning them about where they came from and where they believed their parish of settlement was. This record can provide names for the whole family, sometimes ages, details of where they came from and how they believed they had achieved settlement either in the parish where they were being examined or in another parish.

REMOVAL ORDERS

From 1691 if a settlement examination determined that the person had no right of settlement in the parish and were likely to become a charge on the parish then a removal order was issued and the family was sent back to their original parish of settlement. Some of these removal orders have also survived and can, again, give valuable family detail. The example shown on page 105, the removal of Ezekiel Wilcox from Tipton in Staffordshire to his parish of settlement, Alrewas in the same county, gives the names of Ezekiel Wilcox, his wife Susannah and the names and ages of all of their five children. The document is dated 1833, before the earliest surviving census with national coverage (1841). It is unlikely that you would find this kind of information about the family anywhere else besides the parish chest.

Quarter Sessions records, also held at county archives, might have survived, giving details of disputes over settlement. These can be quite hard to locate unless you have a date because not a great deal of indexing has been done so far. However, if you find any hint of a dispute it would be worth following up.

Where can I find them?

If they have survived, Settlement Examinations, Settlement Certificates and Removal Orders should be found at the county archives for the county to which each parish involved belonged. It is becoming much easier to find them now because many have been indexed. Some indexes are available online or on CD from family history societies. Most county archives will have a copy of any index to papers in their care.

Even if settlement documents have not been indexed they are often not too difficult to search – in fact, if you do end up searching them one by one, the main difficulty lies in bypassing the fascinating stories you find and concentrating on looking for your family name! Survival for some areas is poor but it is well worth the trouble of looking because, if you do find one relating to your family, it can contain information that you simply would not get anywhere else.

PARISH APPRENTICESHIP INDENTURES

Apprenticeships for pauper children were often sought by the parish officers as a means of securing a future for the child. Probably uppermost in their minds, however, was that it was a means of releasing the child into the hands of someone, preferably in another parish, who would pay for their upkeep and give them a place of settlement into the bargain. Within their own parish a certain amount of compulsion was exercised to make people take on apprentices.

A good apprenticeship could be the making of a poor

COUNTY OF STAFFORD. } To the Church-wardens and Overseers of the Poor of the Parish of Tipton, in the County of Stafford, and to the Church-wardens and Overseers of the Poor of the *Parish* of *Alrewas* — in the County of *Stafford* — and to each and every of them.

UPON the Complaint of the Church-wardens and Overseers of the Poor of the Parish of Tipton aforesaid, in the said County of Stafford, unto us whose Names are hereunto set, and Seals affixed, being two of his Majesty's Justices of the Peace in and for the said County of Stafford, and one of us of the Quorum, that *Ezekiel Wilcox — Susannah his Wife and their Five Children namely Ann aged about nine years Joseph aged about seven years John aged about Five years Helen aged about three years and Ezekiel about one year and nine Months* have come to inhabit in the said Parish of Tipton, not having gained a legal Settlement there, nor produced any Certificate owning *them* — to be settled elsewhere; and *have* — become chargeable to the said Parish of Tipton. We the said Justices, upon due proof made thereof, as well upon the Examination of the said *Ezekiel Wilcox*

upon Oath as otherwise, and likewise upon due consideration had of the Premises, do adjudge the same to be true; and we do likewise adjudge, that the lawful Settlement of *him* — the said *Ezekiel Wilcox Susannah his Wife and their said Five Children* —

is in the said *Parish* — of *Alrewas* — in the County of *Stafford* We do therefore require you the said Church-wardens and Overseers of the Poor of the said Parish of Tipton, or some or one of you, to convey the said *Ezekiel Wilcox Susannah his Wife and their said Five Children*

from and out of your said Parish of Tipton, to the said *Parish* — of *Alrewas* — and *them* to deliver to the Church-wardens and Overseers of the Poor there, or to some, or one of them, together with this our Order, or a true Copy thereof; And we do also hereby require you the said Church-wardens and Overseers of the Poor of the said *Parish* — of *Alrewas* — to receive and provide for *them* as Inhabitants of your *Parish* Given under our Hands and Seals, the *Nineteenth* — Day of *February* in the Year of our Lord, 18 *33*.

An order for the removal of Ezekiel Wilcox and family from Tipton, Staffordshire to Alrewas, Staffordshire 1833. (Reproduced by kind permission of Staffordshire Record Office ref D783/2/3/19/348 and the Vicar and Churchwardens of All Saints, Alrewas.)

Know all Men by these Presents that We William Deavill of Great Haywood in the County of Stafford Blacksmith, and Thomas Johnson of the same Place Blacksmith, are held and firmly bound unto Thomas Bailey Churchwarden and Samuel Bakewell Overseer of the Poor of the Parish of Alrewas in the said County, in Trust for the Parishioners of the said Parish in Forty Pounds, each, of good and lawfull Money of Great Britain, to be paid to the said Thomas Bailey and Samuel Bakewell, or their certain Attorney, their Executors, Administrators, or Assigns: To which payment well and truly to be made We bind ourselves our Heirs, Executors, and Administrators, firmly by these Presents; Sealed with our Seals, and dated the Sixth Day of October in the Fifteenth Year of the Reign of our Sovereign Lord George the Third, of Great Britain, France and Ireland King, Defender of the Faith, and so forth, and in the Year of our Lord one Thousand Seven Hundred and Seventy five

The Conditions of this Obligation is such, that whereas Mary Stringer of the Parish of Alrewas in the County of Stafford aforesaid, Singlewoman, in her Examination taken in Writing upon Oath before James Falconer D. D. one of his Majesty's Justices of the Peace in and for the said County, hath declared that on the Eighth Day of April in the Year of our Lord, one Thousand Seven Hundred and Seventy two, at Alrewas, in the Parish of Alrewas, in the County aforesaid, she the said Mary Stringer was delivered of a Female Bastard Child, and that the said Bastard Child is likely to become chargeable to the said Parish of Alrewas, and hath charged the above bound William Deavill with having gotten her with Child of the said Bastard Child. If therefore the said William Deavill and Thomas Johnson

A bastardy bond for the maintenance of the female child of Mary Stringer of Alrewas, Staffordshire, 1775. (Reproduced by kind permission of Staffordshire Record Office ref D783/2/3/17 and the Vicar and Churchwardens of All Saints, Alrewas.)

or either of them, their or either of their Heirs, Executors, or
Administrators, do and shall from Time to Time, and at all Times
hereafter well and truly pay or cause to be paid, unto the said Thomas
Bailey and Samuel Bakewell, or their Successors Church Wardens
and overseers of the Poor of the Parish of Abcevax aforesaid
the Sum of one Shilling and Sixpence weekly and every Week
so long as the said Child shall remain chargeable to the said Parish
then this present Obligation to be void, or else remain and be in
full force and Virtue

William Peavill

Sealed and delivered being first duly
Stamp't in the Presence of

Thos Johnson

: The Word hereafter was Inserted
before the Execution hereof

Joseph Rochford

Benjn Cooper

UNLIMITED SERVICE
ATTESTATION FOR ROYAL MARINES

QUESTIONS, To be separately asked by the Magistrate.	ANSWERS. To be sworn to by the Recruit.
1. What is your Name?	*William Battle*
2. In what Parish, and in, or near what Town, and in what County, were you born?	In the Parish of *Eastry*, in or near the Town of *Sandwich* in the County of *Kent*
3. What is your Age?	*19* Years *10* Months
4. What is your Trade or Calling?	*Laborer*
5. Are you an Apprentice?	*No*
6. Are you married?	*No*
7. Are you ruptured or lame; have you ever been subject to Fits; or have you any Disability or Disorder which impedes the free use of your Limbs, or unfits you for ordinary Labour?	*No*
8. Are you willing to be attested to serve in the Royal Marines until you shall be legally discharged?	*Yes*
9. On what day, and by whom, were you enlisted?*	On the *19 November 1840 by Capt. Jas. Wood RMs*
10. For what Bounty did you enlist?	*Three Pounds —*
11. Do you now belong to the Militia?†	*No*
12. Do you belong to the Army, or to the Marines, Ordnance, or Navy?	*No*
13. Have you ever served in the Army, Marines, Ordnance, or Navy?‡	*No*

I *William Battle* do make Oath that the above Questions have been separately put to me; that the Answers thereto have been read over to me; and that they are the same that I gave and are true.

I do also make Oath, that I will be faithful and bear true Allegiance to Her Majesty, Her Heirs, and Successors, and that I will, as in duty bound, honestly and faithfully defend Her Majesty, Her Heirs, and Successors, in Person, Crown, and Dignity, against all Enemies, and will observe and obey all Orders of Her Majesty, Her Heirs, and Successors, and of the Generals and Officers set over me. **So help me God.**

Witness my Hand,

Sworn before me at *Rochester* this *20* day of *November* One Thousand Eight Hundred and *forty /.*

The mark of William Battle { Signature of the Recruit.

Saml. Parry Copl. Witness present.

Signature of the Magistrate. *William Elwr*

* The Recruit cannot be attested sooner than Twenty-four Hours, nor later than Four Days after his Enlistment.
Clause of Mutiny Act.

† The Magistrate is directed, in putting the 11th Question to the Recruit, and before he receives his Answer, distinctly to apprize the Recruit, that if he belongs to the Militia and denies the fact, he is liable to Six Months' Imprisonment.

‡ If so, the Recruit is to state particulars of his former Service, and the cause of his Discharge, and is to produce the Certificate of his Discharge, if he has it with him.

Attestation papers to serve in the Royal Marines at Chatham 1840. William Battle. (Crown Copyright. Courtesy of the National Archives ref ADM157/33/30.)

9 Serving Their Country – the Records of Fighting Men

Britain had an Empire for a long time. It needed defending and the individuals who had to do that were probably your ancestors.

There are specialist books that concentrate on researching individual branches of the armed forces, so one chapter cannot hope to do justice to the wide range of possible avenues of research. This chapter is weighted towards advice about finding records for those who fought in the two World Wars because that is where the interest of many first time researchers lies. Most people know or can recall knowing a family member who fought in one of them. However, there are some useful pointers to earlier research in general at the beginning, and in relation to individual services towards the end of the chapter.

RESEARCHING THE ARMED FORCES

Why do I need these records?

If your ancestor served his (or, more recently, her) country in time of war, or was part of a peacetime standing defence force, then it is possible that, from the late-eighteenth century onwards at least, records have survived that might contain some detail about him. When he joined there would be attestation papers. The example opposite is of the first page of the attestation papers of Royal Marine William Battle, an unmarried labourer recruited in Rochester, Kent. It shows the kind of questions that new recruits had to answer in 1840. The questions did not change much over the years up to the twentieth century. The answers he gave about his parish of birth and his age can be followed up in parish

registers and, for those born after July 1837, in the General Register Office indexes to births (see Chapter 2).

It is important to remember that people had a wide variety of reasons for joining up. Further research elsewhere would show whether William Battle was telling the truth about his age, for example. If he were an older man you might, in particular, query whether he had been truthful about his marital status or had joined the Royal Marines in order to escape his responsibilities. Some younger men might join up to escape from an unhappy apprenticeship. Their masters had a right to insist on their return but, if they had been shipped abroad in the meantime, there could be a long wait involved! It should be possible to look for other documents in the parish chest (see Chapter 8) and look at the parish registers (see Chapter 6) to check at least some of this out. Now that you have a parish of origin it should also be relatively easy to look for William Battle and his family in the ten-yearly census returns (see Chapter 4). According to information given in the National Archives catalogue William Battle served in the Royal Marines only until 1842 so, unless he was clearly identifiable in the 1841 census, without the papers illustrated you might never know he had been in the armed forces at all.

A second chance of finding further information might come from any surviving discharge papers completed when a man left the forces or from pension records either for himself or his widow. There are large gaps in the files, of course, but at their best records of the army, navy, air force and marines can give a place of birth, a name and address of next of kin, names of children and dates of birth and even a physical description. This is in addition to recording the ups and downs of his career in the armed forces and details of any injuries sustained or illnesses developed during the time of service.

The amount of information you might find depends a great deal on the period in which your ancestor served and whether he was an officer or in the so-called other ranks. Information about officers is usually easier to find. If you do manage to find him mentioned in the ten-yearly census returns (1841–1911) or general certificates of birth, marriage or death (from 1837 to the present) his regiment or ship might be named, but there were no set rules.

People in the armed forces might be difficult to find in other records. They might not appear in census returns if they were serving abroad. Their marriage or death could be recorded anywhere, at home or abroad, depending on where they served. Your only chance of finding personal information about them might lie in paperwork originated by the branch of the armed forces in which they served.

BIRTHS, MARRIAGES AND DEATHS OVERSEAS

In addition to the General Register Office indexes to certificates of birth, marriage and death discussed in Chapter 2, there are separate General Register Office indexes covering births, marriages and deaths overseas. Some of those indexed were inevitably members of the armed forces. There were also separate indexes relating specifically to members of the armed forces. The General Register Office indexes to Armed Forces births, marriages and deaths including Regimental Registers of Births and Baptisms 1761–1924; Army Chaplains' Registers 1796–1880; Army Returns of Births Marriages and Deaths 1881–1955; and

Departments, Series, Items and Pieces at the National Archives

A large proportion of the military archives are held at the National Archives at Kew, London. When you visit them for the first time it takes a while to work out how the cataloguing system works. It is a good idea to access the catalogue online before you go, if you can, and try a few lines of possible enquiry to see how the system works. Some series are better catalogued than others but a big effort has been made to work on the ones that are most in demand, which covers a lot of the documents usually ordered by family historians.

If you do get the chance to look at the catalogue before you go, you can work out a strategy for when you get there and this will help you make the most of your day's research. If you already have a reader's ticket you can order some documents in advance and get off to a flying start.

Look at the National Archives reference for the example given on page 114 – ADM157/33/30.

The **letters** – in this case ADM – at the front of a document reference at the National Archives represent the Government Department that produced them for example ADM for Admiralty, WO for War Office, BT for Board of Trade.

The main groups of **numbers** that you will use represent, first, a **Series**, which is a group of documents with a similar background – in this case ADM157. (Think of it as a filing cabinet within a section of the department.)

Then a **Piece** number, for example 33 is added (perhaps a drawer within the filing cabinet containing boxes or files) ADM157/33. Then possibly but not always there is an **Item** number, for example 30 (to complete the analogy, a file from within the drawer, a piece of paper or a bundle of papers in a box) – ADM157/33/30.

Only **Pieces** or **Items** can be small enough to order, so the sequence of numbers you submit as an order has to be very precise. There are other subdivisions in this hierarchy but if you bear the ones mentioned in mind you will be able to keep track. Once you are signed in to the National Archives system you can keep an overview of what you have seen, and what you have ordered, but it is also very useful to keep a note on paper.

The National Archives uses a standard system of cataloguing and you will find that most other archives' systems are similar in structure even if they use different terms to describe the various parts.

Service Departments Registers of Births and Marriages 1956–1965 are available online for a fee at the Findmypast website along with registered war deaths in the two World Wars and Boer War deaths 1899–1902. Some libraries and archives might also have the indexes on microfiche which you can usually access free.

If you find your ancestor in the indexes you should apply to the General Register Office for a certificate. The early overseas indexes in particular are by no means comprehensive but you might be lucky and find what you are looking for. It helps if you have an idea of where and when the event took place and the name of the spouse or parents. After 1966 the indexes for the Services were combined with others to form a general 'Abroad' category, which is where you should go after that date for information if a search in the UK fails.

For a good general introduction to what you might hope to find in terms of records for births, marriages and deaths see Richardson's *The Local Historian's Encyclopedia* D229–241. Amanda Bevan's *Tracing your Ancestors at the National Archives* gives a simple and thorough guide. The National Archives' Research Guides to individual types of military records are also very helpful. They can be seen online at the National Archives website or are available at the National Archives at Kew, London.

How can I find the records of my military ancestors?

More and more military records are being indexed by name online. However, the indexes do not cover everything. They are also not infallible and for people with common names and little other information, or for people who have tried the indexes and failed, it will pay to know some alternative routes to the documents you are looking for.

Traditionally, the key to a successful search for a military ancestor is finding their regiment or ship in the early years or their identifying service number in the two World Wars. If you have found reference to a military ancestor in other documents but no clues as to which regiment he served with or which ship he served on there are several ways to try to find this information.

Look for a will, which might mention the regiment or ship. Men of all ranks, particularly those who served abroad, made wills and there is no reason why your ancestor should not have been one of them. For wills before 1858 try the Prerogative Court of Canterbury (PCC) wills first (*see* Chapter 5 for more on these wills) or the Wills of Royal Naval Seamen (ADM48 1786-1882). Both are held at the National Archives and are also available through their Documents Online website.

The books in the series *The National Index of Parish Registers* (Society of Genealogists) contain an introduction to each county which names early regiments associated with that particular county.

The online catalogue of the National Archives increasingly contains names of individual servicemen in relation to records held about them in the Archives, so that is definitely worth a look.

Occasionally you will find the name of a regiment or ship on a census return or civil registration certificate (*see* Chapter 4 and Chapter 2).

Any old photographs might give enough detail of the uniform to allow identification. There are specialist books available to help one do this including Neil Storey's *Military Photographs and How to Date Them*. Most large reference libraries will have a copy of a book of this type, or be able to get hold of one for you.

Check if there are any medals in the family. Army medals, for example, should have name, rank, number and regiment. Even the box they came in might be labelled.

World War I army medal cards in series WO372 at the National Archives in Kew, London, are published online and are indexed alphabetically at their Documents Online website. Servicemen received medals for being involved in a particular campaign as well as for gallantry and bravery so it is probable that there will be in existence a medal card for your ancestor if he served in the First World War. They should contain at least a name and service number and information about the type of medal received. Medal cards are not so useful if your ancestor had a common name, unless you have other information to go by such as a middle name. You have to pay to view the cards at Documents Online. Again, if you visit Kew you can see them for nothing.

In 1918, and again in 1919, when the Register of Electors was published, it included men who were still in the armed forces, many of whom might have just been given the vote for the first time. They were listed as

'Absent Voters'. If you know where the family lived during and just after World War I it is possible that you might find your ancestor in this list, along with a 'Description of Service, Ship, Regiment, Number, Rank, Rating &c....' and a home address. The list for Birmingham has been indexed and is available at the Midlands Historical Data website. There are a few other lists available online, including Leeds City Council (for Leeds Absent Voters List). If you type Absent Voters List into a search engine you might be lucky and find one for the area you are looking for. (For more information about electoral registers see Chapter 3.) Lists of Service Voters were also compiled in 1946 after World War II for those who were still in the armed forces. The local library or archives for the area where your ancestor lived should be able to tell you if a list has survived.

For officers you should find their details in the published *Army List, Navy List* and *Air Force List*. All three can be found in reference libraries around the country, at the library of the Society of Genealogists and the library at the National Archives (more details and dates covered are later in this chapter). Some parts of the lists are indexed alphabetically.

Try also *The London Gazette,* now available online and indexed for details of medals awarded and promotions of officers.

A copy of the *Home Guard List* 1939–45 is in the reading room at the National Archives at Kew.

WORLD WAR II AND AFTER

Where can I find the records?
Individual service records of those who fought in World War II and in subsequent wars are still with the Ministry of Defence. Each branch of the services provides a different address to write to – these are given at the back of this book in the Useful Addresses section.

You can download a Request for Service Details form via the Veterans UK website. You need details about the person's service if you know them, along with their service number and/or date of birth which are mandatory. If you are not the person named you are likely to be asked for proof that you are their next of kin or proof that you have their permission to make the request. If

---

Service Records no longer with the Ministry of Defence have been transferred to the National Archives at Kew, London. The exact dates of coverage differ between the services. As a rough guide, the National Archives should hold the records of:

Army Officers commissioned before 1920
Army Other Ranks who enlisted before 1920
Royal Air Force Officers who served before 1922
Royal Air Force Airmen who served before 1924
Royal Marine Officers commissioned before 1926
Royal Marine Other Ranks who enlisted before 1926
Royal Navy Officers commissioned before 1914
Royal Navy Ratings who enlisted before 1924
Women's Royal Naval Service First World War records
(Information from the Veterans UK website – see list)

It is important to note, however, that not all records have survived.

---

this is not the case, for up to twenty-five years after their death, you will only be given minimal information about them. If you do not have access to the internet write to the addresses given to request a form. There is a charge for the search for Service Details, shown on the website. (Note that Veterans UK is there to provide welfare support for armed forces veterans. They are not able to provide a family history research service.)

WORLD WAR II MEDALS

Many people who were in the Armed Forces in World War II were entitled to Campaign Medals. Some did not apply for these so it is possible that an application could still be made by the person themselves or their next of kin. The address to write to is in the addresses section at the end of the book.

Citations for all Gallantry Medals and Awards should be found in the *London Gazette* which is now available online at the Gazettes Online website and through larger libraries and archives – but check by phone before going out of your way to make a visit to a library specifically to see a copy.

WORLD WAR II WAR DIARIES, LOGS AND OPERATIONS RECORD BOOKS

If you are unable to get access to original service records, but you know the unit your ancestor served with, you can still get a flavour of what they were doing on a particular day during the war by looking for the records kept by their commanding officer.

Commanding officers in the Army and Royal Marines were obliged to keep 'War Diaries' – an account of the day-to-day events occurring and actions taken. Not all have survived, and not many names appear in those that have, but they really bring to life the kind of world our ancestors were living in and the pressures they were under. Ships' and Submarines' Logs will give you similar information about naval ancestors' general activities but are unlikely, again, to give details of individual personnel. The RAF Operations Record Books fulfilled a similar function for the RAF.

The amount of detail varies in all of these documents, depending on who wrote them, but sometimes you can find details of people transferred in and out on a particular day or even names of individuals engaged in a particular action. However, as always, it is the officers who are most likely to be mentioned.

All of the above can be found at the National Archives at Kew. Consult their information sheets to get the most out of your visit and check their Documents Online website to see if any of the above records are online.

The names on a village war memorial. (Photo: Tom Ross.)

OFFICERS

Officers, in general, are easier to find than other ranks. *Army Lists (*first published 1740, then annually from 1754*), Navy Lists* (pub. 1782 onwards) and *Air Force Lists* (pub. 1918 onwards) should give you a brief account of officers' careers and dates of changes of rank.

COURTS MARTIAL AND PRISONERS OF WAR

Any surviving documents regarding Courts Martial are held at the National Archives. Also at Kew are documents relating to Prisoners of War (PoWs). Some lists of Prisoners of War are in series WO392 at Kew and its library holds a series of books listing PoWs from all services [shelf ref. 940.5472]. Escape reports for Europe, the Mediterranean and North African theatres are in WO208, with a card index of names available. Ancestry has digital images of records for Prisoners of War held in Germany up to 30 March 1945 available online.

The International Red Cross Archives in Geneva has an incomplete record of PoWs which they will search for you on request. A search can take about six months, according to their website (*see* list) and a fee is usually payable.

THOSE WHO DIED IN WORLD WAR II

Names of soldiers might appear in the Army Roll of Honour, held at the National Archives at Kew series WO304, if they died between 1 September 1939 and 31 December 1946. The roll is also available online, for a fee. It has been indexed – and the transcribed and decoded information is available at the Findmypast website, Military Genealogy and Ancestry. All ranks are included, as are those listed as missing, presumed dead.

The National Archives has a copy of a Royal Marines Museum publication *A Register of Royal Marines War Deaths 1939–1945* by J.A. Good. This covers officers and other ranks. The Royal Marines Museum website has an archives section with some useful information sheets covering all periods of research.

ARMY IN WORLD WAR I

LISTS AND INDEXES

Those who died

There are generally considered to be more research avenues open to people whose ancestors were killed during World War I than for those whose ancestors survived. The best known of these is probably the *Soldiers Died in the Great War* index. This very helpful index has been available on CD for some years and is kept by many libraries and archives. It is also available online at Military Genealogy and Findmypast.

If you know the Regiment then the Regimental Museum may have a Roll of Honour which is likely to include the name of your ancestor. Many businesses, particularly the railway companies, created their own Roll of Honour of their own employees which might be available in company archives or on a memorial at their former place of work if it still exists.

THE COMMONWEALTH WAR GRAVES COMMISSION AND WAR MEMORIALS

The Commonwealth War Graves Commission

The Commonwealth War Graves Commission website, with its Debt of Honour database, is a good starting point if you are looking for a soldier, sailor, airman, or merchant seaman ancestor who died in either of the World Wars. It also lists some civilians. The website for the Commonwealth War Graves Commission can give details such as your ancestor's regiment, rank, his age and/or date of death, service number and details of where he is buried. The amount of information available varies with each entry.

War Memorials

In general the names of those who died in World War II were often added to war memorials built to honour the dead from World War I. Some give a date and location of death which might lead you on to other information. Others give just a name. Work is in progress on a database of all war memorials at the National Inventory of War Memorials. For details see the United Kingdom National Inventory of War Memorials in the list of websites. Local newspapers and church magazines might contain details of service personnel from their area or parish.

The War Office produced Casualty Lists from which names were extracted by local newspapers. Publication was frequent during the early years of the war but less so later on. Early lists contained names of Regiments but this was soon dropped for fear of giving too much away. There was a delay of some weeks between the event and the publication of the list. There are few indexes available, so in most cases it will require a page-by-page search from the date of death.

Selected papers from the National Archives series WO161 containing interviews with World War I prisoners of war, from the Committee on the Treatment of British Prisoners of War, are available online at the Documents Online website.

MEDAL ROLLS AND CARDS

There is a short discussion of the contents of World War I army medal cards at the beginning of the chapter. The cards can be found at Documents Online. The medal rolls, held at the National Archives in WO329 (1917–1936) are unlikely to provide a great deal more useful information.

ARMY OFFICERS IN WORLD WAR I

If the officer you seek continued to serve in the army after 1922 you will have to apply to the Ministry of Defence for information (see above). If he died or left the army before 1922 then you will have mixed results in your search because the main collection of documents relating to army officers in World War I were destroyed by bombing in World War II. Content of the surviving files can vary enormously – from simply a note of a date of death to attestation papers containing personal details. The only way to find out is to have a look.

An index to the officers' files is at WO338 at the National Archives and is available at Documents Online. The surviving papers themselves are in series WO339 and WO374, and are searchable online in the National Archives catalogue by the officer's surname. It will probably help you enormously if you can find details of rank and regiment in the published *Army Lists* before tackling the files.

ORDINARY SOLDIERS IN WORLD WAR I

If your soldier ancestor continued to serve in the army after 1920 you should write to the Ministry of Defence. If your soldier served in the Household Cavalry (including the Life Guards, the Household Battalion and the Royal Horse Guards) their records 1799–1920 should be found in series WO400 at the National Archives at Kew. Other records did not survive intact. Not many of the records for soldiers in the remaining regiments have survived. The National Archives gives a figure of 40 per cent overall. This covers records in two different series, each with a different emphasis.

WO363 – The 'Burnt' Documents
(Documents that survived the effects of an incendiary bomb in 1940)

These are the records of soldiers who survived the war, died in the war or were injured but died before being discharged with a pension.

WO364 – The 'Unburnt' Documents
(Files from the Ministry of Pensions)

These records only relate to soldiers who were discharged with a pension.

Both of these sets of records are available at the National Archives on microfilm and online at Ancestry. Some of them consist of several pages of useful information. Others just give the minimum. If you are looking for a soldier with a common name it is useful to have other information such as age, an address or service number in order to distinguish him from the countless others.

Soldiers' Effects Ledgers
The National Army Museum has a set of 'Soldiers' Effects Ledgers' from April 1901 to March 1960, listing money owing to any soldiers who died in service. They can contain details of the name and regimental number of the soldier, date of death, sometimes the place of death, the name of the next of kin and what money was paid to them. 1901–1914 ledgers might also include the date he enlisted and his trade when he enlisted. These files might prove useful if the documents held by the National Archives do not yield a result.

The museum offers a search service, for which a

moderate fee is payable. In order to do a search and provide a transcript they need to know a name and date of death. The name of the regiment and the soldier's service number are 'useful but not essential'. The address to write to and the National Army Museum website are listed at the end of this book. Similar ledgers for 1862 to 1880/1881 are at the National Archives.

WAR DIARIES AND TRENCH MAPS

If you have tried everything and still drawn a blank you can, if you know your ancestor's regiment, still get an idea of what he might have been doing during the war by consulting the War Diaries and the Trench Maps at the National Archives. Most War Diaries are in WO95 at the National Archives, some of which are available at Documents Online; maps are in WO153.

CHURCH MAGAZINES AND LOCAL NEWSPAPERS AND HISTORIES

Names of those members of the congregation serving or who had died might be found in Church Magazines. Local newspapers printed lists of casualties. Local history books might contain names of members of 'pals' battalions (formed from men from the same towns and

villages who left for war together in 1914 and 1915 and died together, many on the Somme, leaving the area they came from bereft of young men).

THE ROYAL NAVY IN WORLD WAR 1

NAVAL OFFICERS

During World War I and World War II the published editions of the *Navy List* did not tell the full story, for reasons of security. You might find more information by going to the confidential versions of the lists held at the National Archives in series ADM177.

The main series of records relating to naval officers are in series ADM196 at the National Archives at Kew, London. Some of these have been digitized and are available at Documents Online (see their website). The service record of an officer in the Royal Navy is well worth looking for. Information it can give includes dates of promotions and awards and dates he was with each ship. Personal information can include a date of birth and marriage, wife's name and the name and occupation of the officer's father. ADM196 includes some records of officers who continued to serve after the end of World War I. Records of Surgeons 1914–1919 are in series ADM104.

NAVAL RATINGS
The Register of Seamen's Services

If your ancestor was a rating in the Royal Navy during World War I his name should appear in the Registers of Seamen's Services 1853–1923 held at the National Archives at Kew, London in series ADM 188 and ADM139. Both series are available at Documents Online (see website list). The same website also has digital copies of records for World War I of the Royal Naval Volunteer Reserve (ADM337).

The Register page for John Henry Carless VC opposite shows you his date and place of birth, his occupation before joining the Royal Navy, a brief physical description, the names of the ships he served on and details of his service with the Royal Navy, including the reasons he was posthumously awarded the Victoria Cross. These details might lead to other details about the medal, including newspaper reports and also to his birth and death certificates. You might also find him in

---

Ministry of Pensions: First World War Widows' Pensions Forms

An eight per cent chance of success
Series PIN 82 at the National Archives at Kew contains an indexed random sample of around eight per cent of the forms relating to First World War widows' and dependants' pensions for all services. The forms are known to be in a fragile state, but if you are visiting Kew it would be worth a look.

If you are lucky enough to find a form relating to your ancestor, the information available can include name and address, where he served and when and where he was killed or injured. It might also contain the amount of pension that was awarded and for what period of time.

Given that so many service records are missing, particularly from the army, this route is worth trying if you have had no luck elsewhere.

The entry for John Henry Carless VC in the Royal Navy Register of Seamen's Services. (Crown Copyright. Courtesy of the National Archives ref.ADM/188/734.)

the 1901 and 1911 census, possibly with the rest of his family.

MEDAL ROLLS

Medal rolls for ratings who served in World War I are in series ADM171/94–119. The National Archives catalogue divides them alphabetically.

THE WOMEN'S ROYAL NAVAL SERVICE (WRNS)

Records of officers and some ratings in the Women's Royal Naval Service (1916–1931) from ADM318 and ADM336 are available at Documents Online.

THE ROYAL MARINES IN WORLD WAR I

OFFICERS

Records of Officers and Warrant Officers in the Royal Marines who might have fought in World War I are in series ADM196, Records of Officers' Services, at the National Archives at Kew, London. Some of these are available at their Documents Online website (1756–1917). Not all have been digitized. Officers in the Marines, called the Royal Marines from 1802, are included in the *Navy List* (1797 onwards).

OTHER RANKS

Royal Marine Service Records from 1846–1932 are available at the National Archives' Documents Online website (ADM 159). To look for a Marine elsewhere at the National Archives it is useful to know which Division of the Marines or Royal Marines he served with because it was the Division that looked after the paperwork. The three main Divisions were at Portsmouth, Chatham and Plymouth; (there was also a Woolwich Division from 1805 to 1869). During the period of World War I you will find mention of Royal Marine Artillery and Royal Marine Light Infantry. It was not until 1923 that they merged under the collective title of the Royal Marines.

You can make an educated guess at a Marine's Division if you have found records of birth, marriage or death within the vicinity of one of their bases, or if you have found their family in a census return. Another way is to look for him in the medal rolls at ADM171, or if you know the name of any ship he served in you might be able to work out the home port of the ship from the *Navy List* and start looking from there. Failing these, the National Archives has a useful Research Guide *'Royal Marines: How to Find a Division'* that might point you to other ways of finding it from the other documents they hold.

Some of the key records that might yield family information or an idea of where your Marine came from are the Registers of Births, Marriages and Deaths held by each Division (a few covering a period including World War I), attestation papers and discharge books.

Pensions records and records relating to Medals for the Royal Marines are with those of the Royal Navy. Look out for *Tracing your Royal Marine Ancestors* by Richard Brooks and Matthew Little, published in association with the Royal Marines Museum.

THE ROYAL AIR FORCE, THE WOMEN'S ROYAL AIR FORCE, THE ROYAL FLYING CORPS AND THE ROYAL NAVAL AIR SERVICE

Before the formation of the Royal Air Force in April 1918 there were two air services – the army's Royal Flying Corps and the Royal Naval Air Service. Any surviving records of individuals from these services and from the very early days of the RAF are held at the National Archives at Kew, London.

The National Roll of the Great War

Shortly after the end of World War I an ambitious publisher attempted to create a national list containing biographical details of as many as possible of those who had taken part. Over eighty per cent of entries relate to people who survived the war, making it a very valuable source if you are lucky enough to be searching for a survivor from one of the areas covered.

Five of the fourteen volumes cover London. Other parts of the country covered are Southampton, Luton (and parts of Bedfordshire and Hertfordshire), Portsmouth, Manchester, Birmingham, Salford, Leeds, Bradford, Bedford and Northamptonshire. Contributions were made by the people themselves, or their relatives, wherever they happened to be living after the war ended. Details include name, rank and unit, address and some details of the reason for their inclusion, which might give something about their service. Not only soldiers were included – all those involved in combat plus nurses and other war workers can be found in the pages. Whether you find anything is a matter of luck and the accuracy of the information, as always, depends on the person who provided it in the first place.

The National Roll of the Great War can be found on the reference shelves at some libraries and archives and also online at Findmypast.

De Ruvigny's Roll
The Marquis de Ruvigny set out to record personal details, with some photographs, of soldiers, sailors and airmen who died in the First World War. The five volumes include 26,000 people. The majority died early in the war but there are some from the later years. The roll can be found in some public libraries and archives and is also available at Findmypast. The same website also has a database of Royal Naval Division Casualties.

The Royal Air Force – Officers

Series AIR 76 at the National Archives has service records for officers who were discharged before 1920. The records of personnel who remained after that date are likely to be with the Ministry of Defence. RAF Officers' service records 1918–19 are available at Documents Online. Officers were also listed in the published *Air Force List* from 1918.

The Royal Air Force – Airmen

Surviving records for airmen who did not go on to fight in the Second World War should be in series AIR 79 at the National Archives. They are arranged by service number, so if you know what it is this gives you a head start. The National Archives advises using the index in AIR 78 if you do not know the service number.

The Women's Royal Air Force

Women serving between 1914 and 1920 might be found in AIR 80. This series is available at Documents Online.

The Royal Flying Corps – Officers

Surviving records of officers in the Royal Flying Corps 1914–1918 can be found at the National Archives in series AIR 76. The records in AIR 76 are available at Documents Online.

The Royal Flying Corps – Airmen

If your airman was no longer with the RFC by April 1918, his papers, if they have survived, will be with the army documents in series WO373 or WO374 at the National Archives (see the section on the Army in World War I for more detail). If he was still with the RFC when it became part of the Royal Air Force, then the papers will have gone to the RAF and you should look in series AIR 79. Campaign medals for members of the RFC are likely to be with those of the Army in WO372, available at Documents Online.

The Royal Naval Air Service – Officers

The Royal Navy held onto their own records of officers who served between 1914 and the changeover to the RAF in 1918. They are in series ADM 273 at the National Archives and should be found in the National Archives

> Records for officers and airmen who went on to fight in World War II are likely still to be with the Ministry of Defence.

catalogue listed by officer's name. For service after March 1918 go to the National Archives series AIR 76.

The Royal Naval Air Service – Airmen

ADM 188 at the National Archives is the home for records of airmen who served in the RNAS up to April 1918, when the RAF was formed. After that, the RAF kept its own records.

THE ARMED SERVICES BEFORE WORLD WAR I

Most of the records for the army, navy and marines before World War I are held at the National Archives. Increasingly, they are making digital images of the most requested documents available at their Documents Online website, so keep a regular watch for new developments on the site. There is a charge for viewing these online but if you visit the National Archives you can see them for nothing.

As mentioned above, unless you are lucky with one of the online indexes, the further back in time you go the more important it becomes to know your ancestor's regiment or ship (some hints about finding this information are given near the beginning of the chapter). The reason for this is because that is how most of the records are filed. For marines, the name of the administrative division is of importance for the same reason.

FINDING OFFICERS

Officers, in general, are easier to find than other ranks in *Army Lists (*first published 1740, then annually from 1754 and monthly from 1798*)* and *Navy Lists* (pub. 1782 onwards, first as Steel's Navy List). An entry in the *Army List,* for example, should give you, as a minimum, his regiment, rank and date of commission or promotion. You can then use other army lists before and after to try to follow his career. The many abbreviations are explained at the front of the book (*see* page 126).

(iv)

ALTERATIONS.

All Communications regarding Alterations, Errors, or Omissions in this Publication should be verified by real Signature, and addressed as follows :—

THE UNDER-SECRETARY OF STATE FOR WAR,

War Office,

Army List.   London, S.W.

Officers who succeed to peerages, baronetcies, or courtesy titles, are responsible for immediately notifying the same to the Under-Secretary of State for War, in order that the necessary alterations may be made in the Army List and in the official records of the War Office.

EXPLANATIONS.

The Words subscribed to the titles of Regiments, as "Peninsula," "Waterloo," &c. denote the Honorary Distinctions permitted to be borne by such Regiments on their Colours and Appointments, in commemoration of their Services.

The names of Officers on the Supernumerary or Seconded Lists are printed in *Italics.*

EXPLANATIONS OF ABBREVIATIONS.

A.D.C. ....Aide-de-Camp to the Queen.
d. ....On the strength of the Depôt.
e. a. ....Attached to Egyptian Army.
Eq. ....Equerry to the Queen.
h.p. ....Half pay.
i. m. ....Instructors, &c. at School of Musketry.
I. of A ....Instructor of Artillery.
I. of M. .....Regimental Instructor of Musketry.
M. ....In Index denotes that Officer is serving with Militia.
m. ....In Regtl. Lists denotes that Officer is serving with Militia.
m. c. ....Attached to the Military College.
m. c. c ....Certificate, Senior Department, Royal Military College.
m. i. ....Attached to Mounted Infantry, Egypt.
p. ....Certificate of Proficiency, or otherwise qualified as Proficient for higher rank than held by Officer.
p. ....Certificate of Proficiency, or otherwise qualified as Proficient.
(p.) ....Subaltern's Certificate of Proficiency.
p. a. c. ....Passed the Advanced Class.
p.d. ....Serving in Army Pay Department.
(prob.) .....On probation for the Indian Staff Corps.
p.s. ....Passed School of Instruction for higher rank than held by Officer.
p. s. ....Passed School of Instruction.
(p.s.) ....School Certificate for Yeomanry Sub-alterns.
p. s. c. ....Passed the final Examination at the Staff College.
Q.H.P. ....Hon. Physician to the Queen.
Q.H.S. ....Hon. Surgeon to the Queen.

[R] ....Reward for Distinguished or Meritorious Services.
® ....Vacated Reward on appointment to Colonelcy of a Regiment, or on removal to new scale of Retired Pay.
r. ....Recruiting.
Res. ....On the Reserved List.
Res. temp. ...On the temporary Reserved List.
s. ....On the Head-Quarter, General, or Personal Staff.
s.c. ....Student at the Staff College.
S. O. P. ......Staff Officer of Pensioners.
sp. emp. .....Specially employed.
Ⓣ ....Captain or Field Officer of Aux. Forces who has passed the Examination in Tactics laid down for Captains in the Army.
(T) ....Officer of the Aux. Forces who has obtained Special Mention at examination in Tactics laid down for Lieutenants of the Army.
(t) ....Passed the examination in Tactics laid down for Lieutenants of the Army.
u. f. p. ....On unemployed full pay.
V. ....In Index denotes that Officer is serving with Volunteers.
v. ....In Regtl. Lists denotes that Officer is serving with Volunteers.
ⓋⒸ ....Victoria Cross.
Ⓦ ....Medal for Waterloo.
Y. ....In Index denotes that Officer is serving with Yeomanry.
y. ....In Regtl. Lists denotes that Officer is serving with Yeomanry.
* ....Temporary Rank.

ORDERS.

K.G. ....Knight of the Garter.
K.T. ....Knight of the Thistle.
K.P. ....Knight of St. Patrick.
G.C.B. ......Grand Cross ....
K.C.B. ......Knight Commander } of the Bath.
C.B. ....Companion ....
G.C.M.G. ...Grand Cross ....
K.C.M.G. ...Knight Commander } of St. Michael and
C.M.G. ....Companion .... St. George.

G.C.H. ....Grand Cross ....
K.C.H. ....Knight Commander } of the Royal Hanoverian Guelphic
K.H. ....Knight ...... Order.
G.C.S.I. ......Knight Grand Commander
K.C.S.I. ......Knight Commander } of the Star
C.S.I. ....Companion..................... of India.
C.I.E. ....Companion of the Indian Empire.

The monthly *Army List* for February 1886, p.iv, Alterations, Explanations and Abbreviations (pub. The War Office 1886).

Look also for Dalton's *English Army Lists and Commission Registers 1661–1714* and *Hart's Army List 1835–1913*. Hart's list can contain more information than the official lists. In addition to the *Navy Lists* look out for Haultein's *New Navy List 1841–1856*, which might contain more information on war service.

The National Archives, the Society of Genealogists and large libraries and archives are likely to have copies of the above but holdings vary enormously from place to place so check before visiting. Early *Army Lists* are not indexed and some of the earlier copies are harder to find.

There are manuscript lists of army officers at the National Archives in WO64 (1702–1823).

THE ARMY

BEFORE 1660

The English Civil War provides us with a recognizable dividing line in army research. Before the Restoration of the Monarchy in 1660 there was no centralized organization of the army and therefore there were generally no centrally kept records. If an army was required, an army was raised. If it was not required, there was no provision for a standing (or permanent) army. Regiments were often known by the names of the officers who led them.

For suggestions as to where the few surviving documents relating specifically to the army pre-1660 might be found, *see* Amanda Bevan's *Tracing Your Ancestors in the National Archives* and the National Archives Research Guides available at the National Archives website or at the National Archives in Kew, London.

You might also find a mention of so-called volunteer units in local archives, contained in the estate papers of landed gentry and nobility. If you can find a copy of E. Peacock's *The Army Lists of the Roundheads and Cavaliers* you might find an officer who fought in the Civil War, but the chances of finding anything are slimmer if you are looking for records containing the name of an ordinary soldier.

AFTER 1660

Research becomes a little easier after 1660. After this time, during the reign of Charles II, a standing army was established but there was still not much in the way of organization. Up to 1751 regiments still tended to bear the name of their officers, for example Colonel Handyside's Regiment, Colonel Holmes's Regiment and so on. After 1751 things began to change and regiments were given numbers and names such as 17th Light Dragoons or 2nd Foot. There were periodic reorganizations, particularly in 1881 when some regiments merged.

Until 1871 to become an officer you had to buy a commission, so officers were usually of a certain rank or wealth. Ordinary soldiers came from the lower classes and included some criminals. In theory eighteen was the age at which young men could be accepted for enlistment but in practice they lied about their age. Very young boys could enlist as drummers.

Useful places to look

Most of the documents you will want to see are at the National Archives, who have published some excellent research guides to the documents in their care. These are available online at and at the National Archives in Kew, London. Also available for this period are the General Register Office indexes to births, marriages and deaths abroad, which include soldiers. An application for the certificate itself (*see* Chapter 2) should give you more information.

When searching for soldiers for this period in the National Archives look out particularly for 'attestation' papers, completed on joining, and 'discharge' papers, completed on leaving.

Soldiers' Service Documents (WO97 1760–1913) have been earmarked for digitization by the National Archives. They include attestation and discharge papers. They are the papers of ordinary soldiers who became Chelsea Pensioners, so will not usually include those who died or took an early discharge without pension. Many were 'out-pensioners' which meant they received a pension but did not live at the Royal Hospital, Chelsea. Some of their papers are already available at Documents Online and Findmypast.

On a visit to the National Archives, Depot Description Books (WO67 1768–1913) containing descriptions of individual soldiers and further pension records (mainly in WO116 and WO117) are worth looking out for. There is also a card index of deserters on the main floor.

At the National Archives' Documents Online website

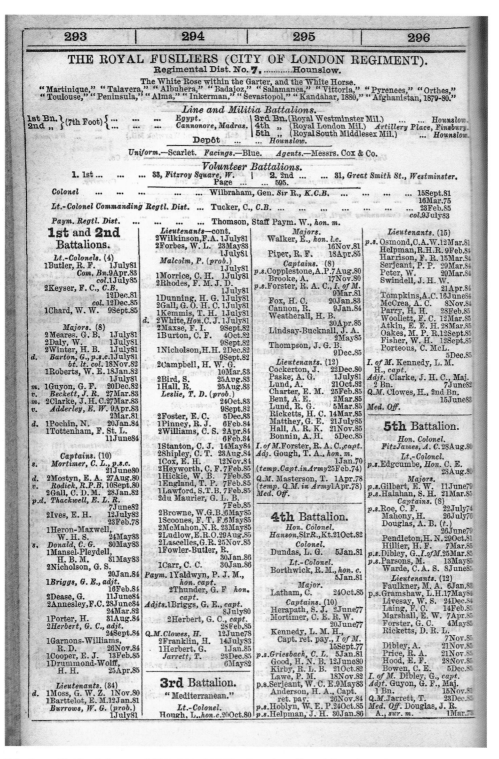

The monthly *Army List* for February 1886, 293–296 The Royal Fusiliers (City of London Regiment), pub The War Office 1886.

is the Waterloo Medal Book MINT/16 which gives the name, rank, corps and regiment of officers and men who fought in the Battle of Waterloo on 18 June 1815. They were eligible to receive the Waterloo Medal – the first medal of its kind to be issued. Searching is free but you have to pay for copies.

Some War Office documents have been released free of charge at Documents Online as part of the National Archives Digital Microfilm project. See the website for further details, and keep an eye out for new developments.

Soldiers are among those groups of people who were more likely to make a will than the population in general. If they died before 1858 look out for a will in the Prerogative Court of Canterbury Wills at the National Archives available, for a fee, at their Documents Online website or for the minimal cost of a paper copy if you visit the National Archives at Kew, London. (This applies to all the documents mentioned above.) For more information on wills before and after 1858, see Chapter 5.

If you can find any of the above documents, or groups of documents, in relation to your ancestor's career it can give you, or lead you to, additional information.

Books such as Amanda Bevan's *Tracing Your Ancestors in the National Archives, Tracing Your Army Ancestors* by Simon Fowler and *My Ancestor was in the British Army* by Michael and Christopher Watts, will give you a great deal of guidance.

THE NAVY AFTER 1660

Like the army, there was no centralized recording system for those who served in the Navy before 1660. You might find senior officers mentioned in general history books or family collections and in a few documents at the National Archives. After 1660 there are records held at the National Archives but not until the nineteenth century are you most likely to find individuals. *Naval Records for Genealogists* by N.A.M. Rodger gives detailed guidance through the wide range of records held in a complicated web of classes. Amanda Bevan's *Tracing Your Ancestors at the National Archives* gives a clear initial breakdown of what is available both before and after 1660 and would be a good starting point.

Tracing Your Naval Ancestors by Bruno Pappalardo is also worth consulting.

Available online are The Royal Naval Officers' Service Records ADM196 (1756–1917), the Wills of Royal Naval Seamen ADM48 (1786–1882) and the Registers of Seamen's Services in ADM188 and ADM139 (1853–1923). All are on the National Archives Documents Online website (*see* list at back of book). There is a fee for this service but viewing is free if you visit the National Archives at Kew. Wills of some servicemen before 1858 are included in the Prerogative Court of Canterbury wills, also held at the National Archives and also available for a fee at Documents Online. After 1858 you should look for wills in the National Probate Registers (*see* Chapter 5). Some records of the Royal Navy are available free at Documents Online, largely un-indexed, as part of their Digital Microfilm project. See the website for details.

Steele's Navy List from 1782 and the official *Navy List* from 1814 provide details of officers serving in the Royal Navy. The amount of information given depends upon when the lists were compiled.

Census returns from 1861 onward list those on board ships on the high seas and in British waters. The General Register Office indexes to registers of naval deaths are discussed earlier in this chapter.

THE MARINES AND ROYAL MARINES

FROM 1755

Through the centuries soldiers had frequently been deployed on ships. In 1665 Charles II formalized the situation by creating a Regiment of Foot specifically to serve on board. After 1690 regiments of Marines were raised when needed for war and then disbanded. At that time they were part of the army establishment and subject to the same administrative structure and regulation.

In 1755 the Marines became a separate entity under the Admiralty. The three main divisions were at Chatham, Plymouth and Portsmouth with an additional division at Woolwich from 1805–1869. Each division looked after administration, so any surviving early records are usually found under the heading of the name of the division.

Where can I find records of Marines?
Officers

There are few original documents relating to officers in the marines before 1793. Advice on how to find early information on officers' careers is contained in the National Archives' research guide on Royal Marine Officers which you can read online or at the National Archives in Kew, London. Series ADM196 at the National Archives contains records of both Naval officers and Marine officers serving after 1793, with an index available in ADM313/110. These records vary but at their best can give very useful information. Not all have been digitized.

Officers in the Marines and Royal Marines from 1802 are included in the *Navy List*, the *New Navy List* and *Hart's Army List* (1835 to 1913). Some of these entries might give retrospective information, particularly *Hart's Army List* and Haultein's *New Navy List 1841–1856*.

Other ranks

Men who were not officers usually stayed with the division they enlisted into, for administrative purposes at least, for the whole of their career.

Records of the Marines (Royal Marines from 1802) are held at the National Archives at Kew, London. Of particular interest will be attestation and discharge papers, description books and registers of service mainly in the series ADM157 to ADM159 and registers of birth, marriage and death mainly in series ADM183 to ADM185. These cover the three main divisions, with some exceptions that can be found in the National Archives' catalogue or the Royal Marines Museum information sheet described below. Records of the Woolwich division are mainly in ADM81.

These are predominantly nineteenth-century records. The National Archives has a card index to attestation records in ADM157 and part of ADM157 is searchable in the National Archives online catalogue by the name of the marine (see the National Archives website for more detail). The Royal Marines Registers of Service in ADM159 are available at the Documents Online website.

The Royal Marines Museum website has an archives section with some useful information sheets covering all periods of research. Look in particular for the Museum Guide Sheet 1 'Tracing RM service records at the National

Archives', which gives the National Archives reference numbers for documents from each division, along with dates covered.

Useful books to look for are *Tracing Your Royal Marine Ancestors* by Richard Brooks and Matthew Little and *My Ancestor was a Royal Marine* by Ken Divall.

THE MILITIA

MILITIA LISTS AND MUSTER ROLLS
Why do I need them?

The militia is frequently described as the Dad's Army of its day but is probably better described as the forerunner of the Territorial Army. Its role changed over the years, depending on whether the country was at war, but it is generally thought of as an occasional defence force, mustered when required. The Statute of Winchester 1285 (Clause 6) decreed that 'every man between fifteen years and sixty be assessed and called to arms...'. The amount of armour and weapons to be provided by each member of the militia depended on his wealth – the poorest were obliged to use 'scythes, gisarmes, knives and other small weapons' (Statute of Winchester quoted in *Tudor and Stuart Muster Rolls* by Jeremy Gibson and Alan Dell). The same book will give you details of where to find surviving documents relating to the early militia.

The militia gained in importance each time the standing army was involved in action overseas. Parish officials would draw up a list of men of the right age for the militia and a ballot was often held to choose those who had to serve. Forces for each county were periodically mustered, or gathered together, for inspection and training. Unless men could afford to pay someone to do their stint for them, they had to do it. Some of these lists, from the parish chest, still survive in county archives but there are also some at the National Archives along with muster records.

Militia lists can just be lists of names, depending on the period you are looking at, but can also contain information about occupations or the number of children, particularly if there was a worry that service in the militia would leave the children dependent on the parish. They might at the very least tell you that a man of the same name as your ancestor was resident in the named parish and of an age to serve.

The importance of the militia fluctuated but by 1757 a Militia Act re-established regiments of militia for each county. From this time onwards you are more likely to find information. *Militia Lists and Musters 1757–1876: a Directory of Holdings in the British Isles* by Jeremy Gibson and Mervyn Medlycott is an excellent guide to what has survived. Survival in some counties is better than in others but the county archives for the county you are interested in should be able to tell you what they have.

The library at the National Archives at Kew, London, has some published militia lists for the eighteenth and nineteenth centuries. The Society of Genealogists has some in its library as well.

WO68 at the National Archives contains records of the Militia 1759–1925 including description books, enrolment books and pay lists and some birth, baptism and marriage registers. You might find details of officers here also. Militia Attestation Papers 1806–1915 in WO96 at the National Archives have been earmarked by the National Archives for digitization. The Origins Network website has an index of Militia Attestations from WO96 1860–1915 from which originals can be ordered. There are some muster rolls in WO13 at the National Archives. Check their online catalogue for details.

And finally – Where do I go from here?

It can take some time to find and to unravel the information contained in the records of fighting men and women, so it is something that people usually investigate alongside their other, more general, research – particularly if they have to pay a visit to the National Archives at Kew, London. A visit to Kew is always a good idea in any case because the documents available online are a very small proportion of what they hold in the archives.

When you do find some information be sure to check it against what you already have, to make sure that the soldier, sailor, marine or airman you have found is the person from the parish and the family you are looking at. This is very important if he has a common name. And keep on looking at military records – if you find one thing you might find more in a different series of documents at the National Archives – until you feel you have genuinely exhausted this avenue of research.

It is vital, too, to get to know as much as you can about any campaigns or action that your ancestor was involved in. There are a great many books available on particular campaigns or particular regiments or naval actions.

As you would do with your other research, check out all the leads you are given and make no assumptions – remember that some people lied about their age to join up, and they might have used an alias to cover this up.

Much of what is available online for a fee can be accessed free. A visit to the National Archives will give you free access to their digitized images. And local libraries and archives might have signed up to a commercial online provider such as Ancestry or FindmyPast. If they have, you should be able to book a session on one of their computers either free or for a small fee.

The military played an important part in our history and military service probably played a larger part in our ancestors' lives than we realize. The fact that the military establishment, particularly in the last two centuries, liked to write things down can only be to our advantage.

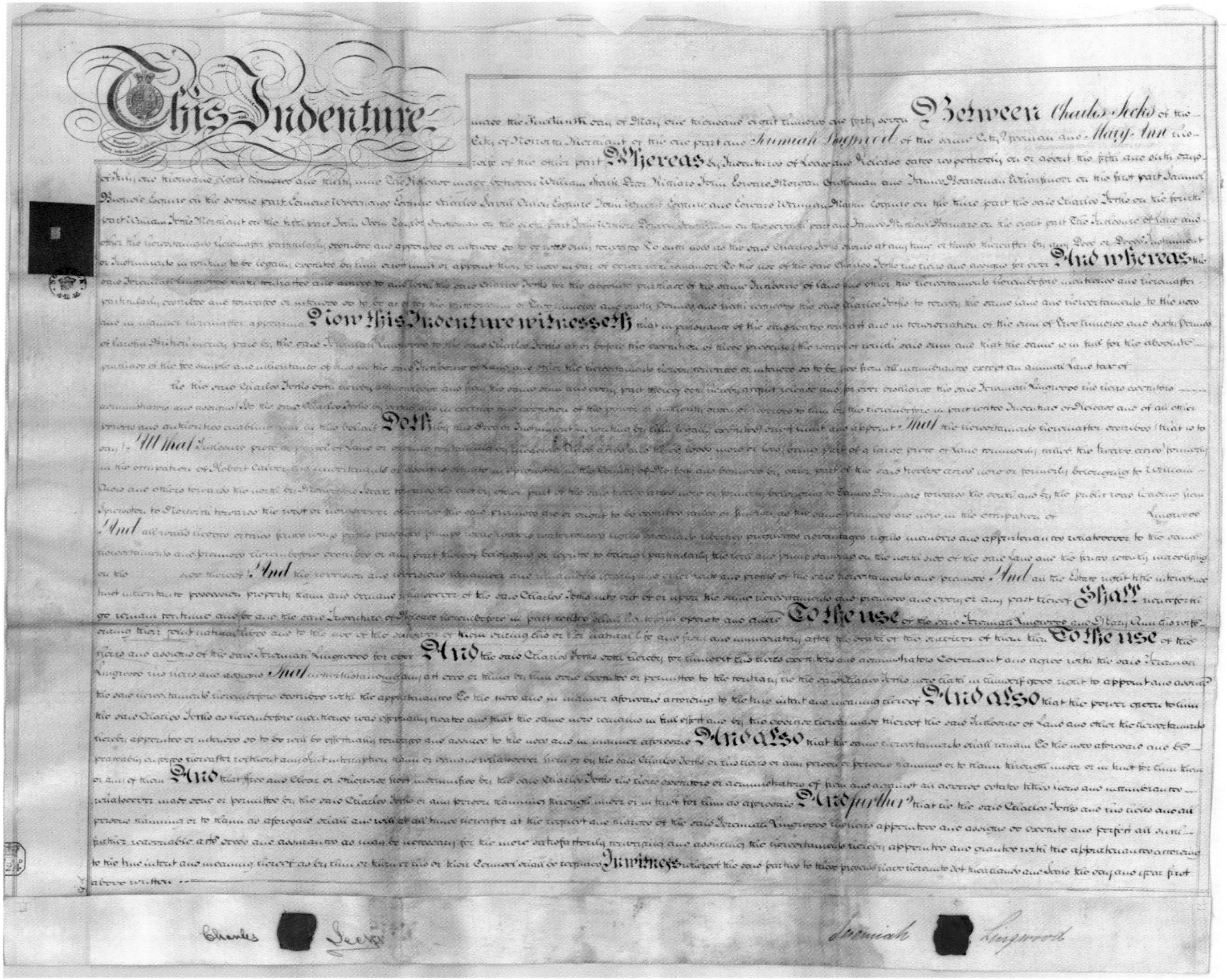

1847 Indenture relating to Conveyance of Land.

10 'Access2Archives', Maps, Property and Land

ACCESS2ARCHIVES (A2A)

Access2Archives is a database available through the website of the National Archives. It has been developed over the past few years to increase the possibility of finding documents for all types of historical researchers however far they are based from the archive holding the documents. Gradually archives all over England and Wales have been putting details from their catalogues online, including the names of some of the people mentioned in the documents. This gives us a chance, from a distance, to search the catalogues of archives for instances of the family name we are looking for and/or the village where they lived.

If you examine the catalogues of any archive, including the National Archives, you will find that some parts of the catalogue go into great detail about what is contained in a particular section and some do not. The catalogue information transferred to Access2Archives is much the same, so by searching the database you are relying to a certain extent upon a lucky find but your chances of coming across something relevant to your search are vastly increased by the existence of A2A.

If your family name is a common one you will need other information to limit your search but if the family name is unusual your chances of a 'hit' being in some way relevant are fairly good. By typing a name into A2A you can come across title deeds, family papers in solicitors' collections and bundles of correspondence among other items. Drafts of wills that never went to probate, mortgage documents and even a rare marriage settlement might come to light.

An estimated thirty per cent of archival catalogues for England and Wales are included in Access2Archives. There is no plan at present to add any more. The details of holdings in a particular archive are not necessarily complete and you should also check the websites of individual archives where you should find more information about what documents they have and how to access them.

THE NATIONAL REGISTER OF ARCHIVES

Other archival indexes of documents online include the National Register of Archives, also accessible via the National Archives website. This is always worth a look but the details given on the site stress that it generally does not contain detailed information of the kind that is of most use to family historians. The families and estates section and the diaries and personal papers might be of interest, particularly if your family took a prominent part in British public life, or if you are looking for papers relating to a particular estate. It is searchable by place, business or personal name.

Neither database contains images of original documents. They are simply a very good means of knowing whether a document relevant to your search might be in an archive somewhere, waiting to be examined. More information is available on the National Archives' website.

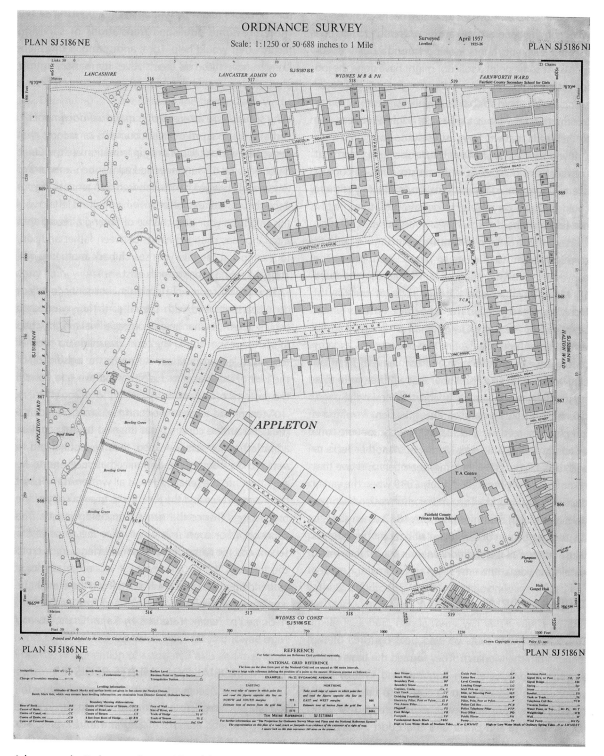

A large scale Ordnance Survey Map (Plan SJ 5186 NE. 1958) of part of Widnes showing the amount of detail that it is possible to see. Scale 1:1250 or 50.688 inches to 1 Mile.

'extracts compiled 1582', to the appointment of a steward in 1933.

The index to some counties in England and all of Wales is available to search online at the National Archives website. The whole register is available to search at the National Archives.

MAPS

Why do I need them?

A family historian without a map to hand is only half equipped. Many people starting their family history lose out by not realizing the value of a good map. At the very least, the index to a modern day road atlas or A–Z can be a help in finding the general area where your ancestors lived. Most helpful, though, are maps made as near to the time of your ancestors as possible.

How can they help me?

Maps can help you to see the best road or footpath to the nearest market town where they might have gone to register a birth or death. Maps will allow you to pinpoint possible places of worship. The parish church might not have been the nearest, most convenient, place to get to on a Sunday. For example, with seven or eight children under ten to walk there and back, your ancestors might have picked the nearest church or chapel to make a hard life a little easier. You might spot on a map a nearby nonconformist chapel, for example, that had a short life and whose registers might not have survived. If your ancestors have gone missing this may be little comfort – but at least it is a possible reason why you cannot find their baptisms in the parish registers.

In large towns and cities families often tended to gather in clusters. A good map and a copy of the census or a carefully kept parish register will help you to pinpoint the particular households. Even if you have no other clues than a surname to suggest that they are related it gives you a starting point to look, perhaps, for marriages and the names of witnesses at those marriages – and for the names of people reporting births and deaths. Obviously, if the census gives them all a similar place of birth you are probably onto a winner. But life is not always that easy. A cluster of Smiths born and living in a small area of London presents you with difficulty. Delve further into the lives of those Smiths living closest to each other, however, and you might be lucky enough to see a pattern.

Occupations can also help to pinpoint your family on a map. A mine or ironworks nearby to provide jobs for a mining or ironworking family means that even if they moved, they might not have moved far away because people walked to work. Draw an imaginary circle around a source of employment and you might still find them in the area.

MAPS AND MIGRATION

Maps enable you to follow with your fingertip the routes that your ancestors might have travelled from the place they were born. Look for what rivers, canals and railway lines passed through the town or village, offering an easier mode of travel out of the place than roads, which were often unkempt. The various Acts passed to enable the building of the canals and railways also generated maps showing the names of landowners.

It is something of a myth that people did not move in

The canals provided a way to migrate, either by water or on foot. (Photo: Tom Ross.)

Monumental or Memorial Inscriptions can provide you with additional information about a family. (By kind permission of the Vicar and Churchwardens of St Mary Magdalene, Tanworth in Arden, Warwickshire. Photo: Tom Ross.)

11 Other Sources

Even though the sources in this chapter have little relation to each other, you should seriously consider them an important part of your search. As was mentioned at the beginning – there was no Master Plan in terms of where we might find the best information to help us with our family history, and therefore no neatly outlined compartment into which to drop these last few suggestions.

MONUMENTAL OR MEMORIAL INSCRIPTIONS

Why do I need to look at them?
Monumental or memorial inscriptions in a churchyard or public cemetery can give additional information about a person, and his or her family relationships, to add to that in an entry in a parish or other burial register, or on a death certificate. They are always worth looking for.

Even the very existence of a gravestone can tell you something about the family. Particularly in the early years, from the late seventeenth century onwards, if your family was able to afford a gravestone with an inscription then they must, at least temporarily, have had money to spare from that spent on scraping a living from day to day. If there is a family memorial inside a church then it usually means that the family had some wealth and/or standing in local society at the time the memorial was built. The same obviously applies to the construction of a family vault.

Where can I find them?
Monumental Inscriptions, or M.I.s as they are sometimes called, can be found on the gravestones and memorials in the burial grounds of parish and nonconformist churches and municipal cemeteries. However, it is not always necessary to go wandering through the grave-yards in search of fading and moss-covered inscriptions on gravestones. It is becoming more and more possible that family history societies will have got there before you and recorded and indexed the M.I.s, particularly those in churchyards. Many of the larger urban cemeteries have yet to be indexed.

Some monumental inscriptions were copied down by volunteers as early as the nineteenth century if gravestones were removed to make way for development – a new railway for example. If this has been done it will usually have been deposited with the county, town or city archive for the place where the grave is situated.

The Society of Genealogists has copies of a great many transcriptions of M.I.s. The family history societies who did many of the transcriptions will often have copies for sale on CD or will look up a name for you for a small fee. So search out their websites using the Federation of Family History Societies' website as a starting point.

Where are they now?
Other family members who are not actually buried where a family grave or memorial plaque is located might also be remembered in the inscription.

The example on page 144 gives the name and regiment of Edward Algernon Ernest Muntz, and the names of his parents. His death at Poona in 1893 is remembered but he is not buried in the grave marked by the stone. The idea of bringing someone's remains home to be buried is a relatively modern one.

CEMETERY REGISTERS

If you have the death certificate, for a town or city dweller in particular, and you cannot locate the burial of your ancestor in a local churchyard, it is possible that he

People who died abroad, or in another part of the country, might still be remembered in their local churchyard. (By kind permission of Mr and Mrs F.D. Muntz and the Vicar and Churchwardens of St Mary Magdalene, Tanworth in Arden. Photo: Tom Ross.)

or she was buried either in a privately developed cemetery or what is now commonly known as a municipal cemetery. A death announcement or the report of a funeral in a local newspaper might tell you where.

Many of the early cemeteries date from the early to mid-nineteenth century, opened to deal with the problem of overflowing graveyards in the inner cities. There was simply no more room to bury people. A prime example of this was the burial ground at St Martin's, the ancient parish church of Birmingham. As early as 1780

the historian William Hutton had written that the churchyard of St Martin's Church:

Through a long course of internment, is augmented into a considerable hill…The growth of the soil causes a low appearance to the building, so that instead of the church burying the dead, the dead would have in time buried the church.

(William Hutton, 1780, from *In the Midst of Life* by Joseph McKenna)

Even then it took over fifty years before a separate cemetery was built for Birmingham.

A few burial grounds were built by nonconformists. For example Bunhill Fields in London was opened privately in the eighteenth century to accommodate their needs (*see* Chapter 7).

Cremation is comparatively new. It became legal in the late-nineteenth century but even by the mid-twentieth century only about ten per cent of people were cremated. Most crematoria keep their own records so you should apply to them if you think your ancestor was cremated.

Where can I find them?

Some of the earlier registers, or indexes to registers, of privately created and municipal cemeteries are with the relevant local and county archives. That would be the first place to make enquiries because if they do not have them they, or a local public library, are likely to have contact details for cemeteries and crematoria within their area. You might also find this information on the local council's website.

Many registers are located at the cemeteries themselves and it is there that you might have to make enquiries. Obviously, if the cemetery is still in use then the priorities of staff will lie with bereaved families and the funerals taking place in the present. Most are very sympathetic to family history enquiries but some have little time available to deal with them. Make your enquiry as clear and simple as possible, giving as much detail as you can – particularly the name and date of death, and wait patiently for an answer. While asking about your ancestors, ask also for the names and details of other people in the same plot. These will not necessarily be family members but, if you don't ask, a golden opportunity to find another possible relative's grave will be lost. The amount of information available can vary enormously from a name, age, address and cause of death to very little more than a name, depending largely on when the burial took place.

You might be charged a fee by the cemetery for a member of staff to look at their registers for you, so it is important to have a very clear idea what you want to achieve from the enquiry. If the fee is quoted as so much for the first half an hour, it is a good idea to wait until you have a handful of people's dates of death before asking whether they are buried at the cemetery. If you then write a letter or email (whichever they prefer) listing your requests in order of priority you can ask them to do as much as they can in the half hour available. The time taken is likely to include the time spent reporting back to you.

Finally, if you are able to look at an index yourself, at the local library or archive, make a note of every number and what column it was in, and also every mark or initial and the date. It may not mean anything to you but it might be the answer to the one question the cemetery will ask when you apply for further details.

A relatively new development is the Deceased Online website, which gives access to some of the burial and cremation records held by local authorities. There is a searchable index to burials from 1837 onwards and a clear list of the local authority databases which are included. The site is expanding so it is worth returning to see what has been added.

OCCUPATIONAL RECORDS

Once you have found out what your ancestor did for a living there might be a record with the business they worked for, in an official professional list or in company records deposited with the relevant county or local archives.

LISTS

Printed lists exist of people engaging in various occupations.

Crockford's Clerical Directory

If your ancestor was a clergyman in the Church of England you should find him listed in Crockford's. Since 1858 this publication has listed all Anglican clergy along with biographical details including where they studied, the year they graduated and a list of parishes where they had worked until the directory was published. Many larger reference libraries have copies.

Army, Navy and Air Force Lists

These list officers only. *See* Chapter 9 for more information.

There are as many different ways of filing and storing your paper information as there are people researching their family history. (Photo: Tom Ross.)

12 How Do I Know When I've Proved It?

At the risk of telling you what you already know, at a very basic level, the way you work at your research can make the difference between being clear and confident in your efforts or being unsure whether you have what you need to prove the links in your family tree.

MAKING NOTES

Where were you when you did this?

While you are doing your research get into the habit of always making a note of which documents you have consulted at a particular archive or online, even if you have found nothing in them to interest you. You should note when and where you found a particular document (put the date at the top of the page, and note the name of the archive or website), the name or title given to the document or series of documents, the exact dates you have searched between, page numbers if present and the document reference number. This should prevent you from looking at the same documents twice and also give you the power to write to an archive and ask them to send you a copy of something if you later decide you need one. It also means that anybody reading your notes can go straight to that document in the archive where you found it.

What was that name again?

When you are making a note of people's names from original documents, and also when you are transferring the name to your family tree, always note the name exactly as it is written in the original document that you consulted, for example Wm should not be expanded to William, even though you are fairly sure that is what it means. Then later, if there is any doubt, you know with certainty what was written and you will not have to go back and check. It can save you a lot of time.

If you find a forename or surname spelled several different ways use the exact spelling you have found in each document when you add each individual piece of information to your accumulated files. This applies to place names too. Don't be tempted to alter any of them; this gives you a good range of possible alternatives to look for in indexes and in other documents at a later date. The more accurate your notes are about how your ancestor was named or described in various documents the easier you will find it to recognize him or her, and to prove that this is, indeed, the person you are looking for.

The end of the line...

If you transcribe a document, put the line endings in your text in the same place as they are found in the original (numbering the lines can be helpful here). Mark any gaps in what is written and any places where you cannot read the writing. If you are having difficulty deciphering it, by far the best thing to do, if possible, is to get a photocopy or digital copy and take it home to read. (For more on reading old documents *see* Chapter 5.)

When searching for a particular name, make a note of the name you have searched for and also the variants of the name that you have searched for, for example Smith(e) and Smyth(e). If you are looking down entries in a parish register for names, record all instances of that name unless you are looking for a very common surname in a large register. Then you will probably have to refine your search but make a note of the fact that you have refined it – something like 'Mary Smith (and variants) and Mary Ann Smith (and variants) only noted; other Smiths present.' You will not remember later exactly what you did look for unless you have made a note at the time. If it becomes important later, you can go back and look for your 'other Smiths'. Also, note any missing years, days or months – perhaps the register has been damaged by water or fire – or illegible entries. This might provide you much later with a possible explanation for why you cannot find the person you are looking for. You can always check to see if these periods are covered by a Bishop's Transcript (see Chapter 6). Also use a new sheet of paper for each new surname – otherwise, when you get it home where are you going to file it?

FROM A DISTANCE…

Even allowing for the increase in documents available online, the progress of your research might mean eventually visiting a part of the country where you have never been before. If so, make a holiday of it if you can, but also leave plenty of time available for research – it always takes much longer than you think. Check with the library or archive that they actually have the documents you would like to consult covering the period of time you need to see, and check opening hours or make a booking if they say you should.

If you cannot visit the particular library or archive that you believe might hold documents relating to your family then see if you can get a family member who lives nearer to go for you, or consider employing a professional researcher to do this particular task for you. Some family history societies have 'research exchange' schemes whereby members unable to travel can do research for each other. If you need copies of something for which you have dates and a reference, most archives are happy to supply it by post; they may also let you know first how much the cost would be.

If you are unable to get to the records for one branch of the family, consider looking at another closer to home and save the ones furthest afield for when you have more free time. The joy that many people derive from their hobby comes from getting to know the area where their ancestors lived – and while you can learn a lot from books and the internet there is nothing quite like visiting the area yourself to get the feel for where your roots lie.

You might find that someone else has already done research that relates to your family. That can be good news and bad news. If you are lucky enough to find this, don't be afraid to read the research critically. One of the key rules of genealogy is to test every finding and try as hard to disprove your pet theory as you do to prove it.

That should apply to other people's work as well as your own. You do not have to fall out with them over it. If you do find a potential hole in their research you can tactfully suggest your own findings as an alternative possibility. It will then be up to them, similarly, to test your theories!

FILING

Now where did I put that?

It could be said that there are as many ways of filing your notes and photocopies as there are people researching their family history. Don't make the mistake of thinking you will suddenly become a neat and tidy filer of documents if you have not been that way to date. If you usually shove everything into a shoe box then use that system but try to improve on it by having a labelled shoe box for every branch of the family that you are researching, and using some coloured dividers or sticky labels to bring a little order to it. If, on the other hand, you like a neat row of A4 ring binders, then that is the way to go. Or if a card index sitting on your desk gives you the greatest reassurance then adopt that system – or use a combination of all three! The whole point is to use something you are comfortable with and something that will enable you to retrieve what you are looking for.

There are computer programs that can help with this, of course, but even if you put all your research onto computer you will still need a way of filing any paper copies of original documents you might come across. If you transfer your notes onto computer do back up your work onto disc or a memory stick. It is also a good idea to let other members of the family have copies of your findings from time to time so that if disaster strikes something might be retrievable.

Filing logic

At its most simple – if you know the names of all your grandparents it is a good idea to start with four files, one for each surname. You could then give each line a colour and use it to mark the files, boxes, pages or index cards. You could even use the coloured printer paper that is readily available – usually in at least four colours to a packet. Then once your research takes off into other lines and your file gets full it is an easy matter to split what you have and allot another colour or combination of colours. Some people prefer to do the same kind of thing using

SOCIETIES AND COURSES

Family History Societies

It is a good idea to join a family history society – in particular one related to the area where you are doing most of your research. Even if you are unable to attend meetings there will usually be a magazine and access to a website and other information. Some societies publish books, transcribe and index registers and some also operate a 'research exchange' system where members will go and look something up in the area where they live in exchange for you looking up some information near where you live. Details of a society near you can be obtained from the Federation of Family History Societies.

The Society of Genealogists

The Society of Genealogists in London, founded in 1911, holds a vast stock of published and unpublished genealogical material in its library which is open free to members, and to non-members for an hourly up to a daily fee. Depending on the type of item required, the library will sometimes lend research materials to members who cannot attend in person. They also publish some of the best books on genealogy and a quarterly magazine with articles written by people who really know their subject. Membership brings seventy-two hours unlimited access to Society of Genealogists material published on Origins Network every quarter.

The Society is open to everyone to join. It is particularly useful for the period before the start of civil registration in 1837 but also has an open access area allowing use of the main family history websites.

Courses

There are a lot of courses available for budding family historians, from beginners' classes to more advanced studies of particular aspects such as manorial documents or the use of maps. You can learn a lot and also talk to people with similar interests and discuss difficulties and ways of getting around them. You can find evening classes at colleges of education, day and half-day courses at the Society of Genealogists and the Institute of Heraldic and Genealogical Studies and lectures at the National Archives. The University of Strathclyde offers a Postgraduate Certificate and a Diploma in Genealogical Studies, Keele University has a Latin and Palaeography Summer School and the IHGS offers correspondence courses leading to varying levels of certification. There are also conferences held around the country, with lectures by experts in their field, and many family history fairs also offer lectures as part of the experience. Look for advertisements in the family history magazines or your local newspaper to find more of what is on offer.

numbers and letters – again, use what you are comfortable with in whatever combination you find the easiest.

In terms of who to file where, if you have to split files to make space, then logic dictates that you file married women under their maiden name if you know it, but cross-reference to their married name or names as well.

For every fact that you enter into your filing system note the source it came from and the reference number. Memory cannot be relied upon! Good filing can.

ARCHIVAL STANDARD STORAGE

You might see advertised some archive standard plastic sleeves for holding your copies of documents. These are excellent but can be quite expensive if you buy a lot of

them. A good compromise, if you are tempted down this route, is to use them for original documents and photos that you might still have in the family – for things that really are irreplaceable. Second priority might be for copies of birth, marriage and death certificates because they would be expensive to replace. However, it should still be possible to get copies of these and any other documents you have obtained through archives, should they deteriorate to any extent.

DRAWING UP YOUR FAMILY TREE

Hours of endless fun – or hours of frustration?

There will come a time when you want to gather together all your notes and draw up a clear copy of your family tree. Many of us draw rough, working copies to help in research, so it is possible you will have a good idea how it will look well in advance.

There are many different ways that you can lay out your family tree. The one that most of us are familiar with from history books is a 'line' tree or pedigree – a deceptively simple method that can cause some frustration. Although even the experts disagree about certain symbols there are certain fundamental rules regarding layout:

- The most important thing is to try to keep members of the same generation on the same line.
- Try not to let the lines cross while drawing your tree – it looks awful and can be misinterpreted. There's usually a way round it.
- When drawing your tree only include people and information that you have checked out thoroughly and believe to be true. For a 'working tree', when only pen and pencil were available for the purpose it was easy to use pen for things that you were certain of and pencil for those that were less clear cut. Now that there are computer programs you have to find another way of indicating uncertainty, either through a note or a '?'.
- It is a good idea to get into the habit of putting surnames in capital letters so that confusion does not arise over names that can be used either first or second for example James THOMAS or Thomas JAMES.
- Children should always be noted in order of birth. If you could improve the layout by altering the order in which they are shown, just number the children in the correct order and then move them around to suit the layout. First and second wives and husbands should be numbered too.
- There is no perfect way to record all the information, but be consistent in the way you record, and distinguish between, births and baptisms in particular (b. for birth, bapt. for baptism makes the distinction).

No matter which method you use, you will end up with several pieces of paper (or even a long roll of wallpaper!) but as long as you clearly mark and number the continuation sheets it will convey the information you want to get across to succeeding generations.

Your 'working tree' will look very different from the ones in the history books. It will be top-heavy as you collect more and more people. There will be ancestors clinging onto the sides and top of the pages, and there will be rubbing out and starting again. Date each effort you make so that you can go back and check that you have not made a mistake. Even if you are using a computer to build your tree, it is a good idea to consult one of the recommended books about layout.

Bear in mind that this pedigree might be consulted by other people when you are no longer around to explain what you meant. You owe them a clear picture of your findings.

Good indentations

Another way of recording your family is to use an indented family tree, similar to the one from Debrett's shown on page 17. Each succeeding generation is noted, in order, further away from the left hand margin. This has the advantage of allowing you to get more people and information onto one page. If you find your layout a bit difficult to follow it can help to colour each generation with a coloured pencil so that you can distinguish them easily – or if your coloured ink cartridge will stand the strain you could do it with your printer.

The Society of Genealogists has an excellent factsheet discussing different ways of recording your family tree. There are also books on the subject including Patrick Palgrave-Moore's *How to Record Your Family Tree* and *Family trees: a manual for their design, layout and display* by Marie Lynskey.

BOOKS AND MAGAZINES

Read all about it!

The range of books on family history now available is quite staggering. Some of the most useful ones are listed in the Bibliography. Many are available online through family history societies, some of which sell through the GENfair website. A good beginners' book is a must. After that your research will dictate which areas you want to know more about. In addition, Mark Herber's *Ancestral Trails* is a very highly regarded and detailed guide to sources available. Most public libraries will have a copy in their reference section or will be able to order it for you. The National Archives publish some

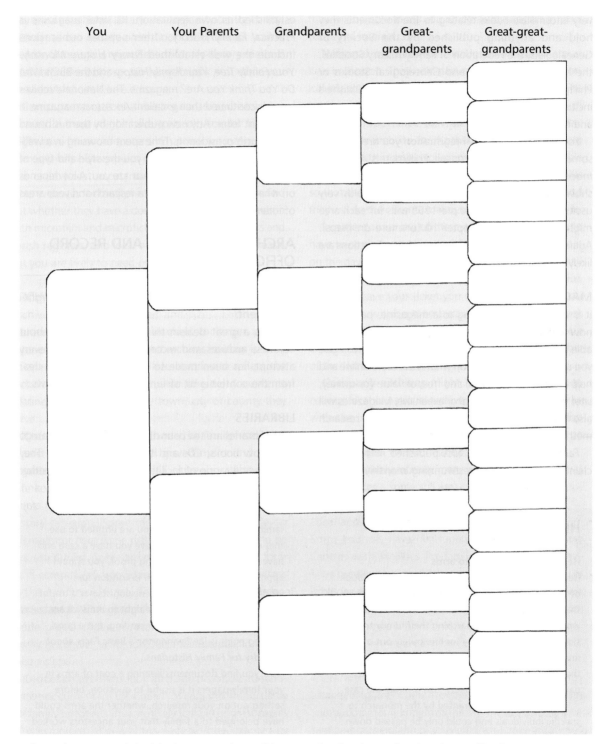

You	Your Parents	Grandparents	Great-grandparents	Great-great-grandparents

Take a photocopy of the blank page and pencil in some details of your family – dates of birth, marriage and death if you know them, or names of brother, and sisters. It is a working sheet so the spaces are left clear for you to use as you would like. It will help you to work out where you would like to start.

Be prepared to let go!

You might have done a lot of work on one line of the family – then find a will or another document that stands your whole theory on its head and proves you wrong. In these cases it can be hard to discard all that hard work and start again – but you must do it in order to preserve the integrity of your family tree.

Keep the work you have done, but label it clearly as a line that went wrong. One day it might be useful to someone else from another branch of the family.

you see a person's name on a list, and nothing else, it does not necessarily tell you that that person was your ancestor – it just tells you that someone with the same name might have been in the area at the time. That is why the documents that do give family information are so important.

Our ancestors, like us, did not always tell the truth to those in authority. They would probably regard the questions of officialdom as intrusive – 'none of their business'. So be a bit streetwise and don't fall into the trap of believing a slender connection just because it is the only one you can find.

Weigh the evidence you have carefully and always look for corroboration. Keep working back and forth over the generations. A piece of evidence you find in the eighteenth century might be capable of corroboration in documents from the nineteenth, in another branch of the family. A will from a branch of the family you did not previously know was yours might refer to an earlier will mentioning your ancestors. Good research does not only go in one direction.

Tracing your family history is a very enjoyable hobby, but it is a hobby with consequences. If you don't get it right, or don't make it clear in your notes where you are unsure or have made a mistake, then your children and grandchildren might pick up your work, mistakes and all, and believe it to be true. What will come with experience is the ability to judge whether you have enough evidence to move back a generation. If you are in any doubt then the answer is that you probably have not accumulated enough to be sure that it is worth all the time and effort you will put in on researching earlier generations. There will always be that nagging feeling in the back of your mind that a particular link is weak and capable of being challenged. Work on it more, move on to something else for a while or recognize that that particular line has gone as far as it is going to go.

Above all, keep a sense of proportion. We all have to recognize that there are some things we are just not going to be able to prove – and that, realistically, if we assemble a mountain of documentary evidence, even the best of us can't cater for those moments 'behind closed doors' that only two people knew about!

Further Information

ALPHABETICAL LIST OF WEBSITES

A Church Near You www.achurchnearyou.com

Access2Archives (A2A)
www.nationalarchives.gov.uk/a2a

Ancestry www.ancestry.co.uk

Archon Directory www.nationalarchives.gov.uk/archon

Association of Genealogists and Researchers in Archives
www.agra.org.uk

Association of Professional Genealogists in Ireland
www.apgi.ie

Association of Scottish Genealogists and Researchers in
Archives www.asgra.co.uk

Association of Ulster Genealogists and Record Agents
www.augra.com

Beamish Living Museum www.beamish.org.uk

The Black Country Living Museum www.bclm.co.uk

BMD Index www.bmdindex.co.uk

BMD Registers www.bmdregisters.co.uk

The Borthwick Institute www.york.ac.uk/inst/bihr

British Association for Adoption and Fostering
www.baaf.co.uk

British History Online www.british-history.ac.uk

British Library www.bl.uk

British Library Newspaper Images
www.imagesonline.bl.uk

Castle Garden, New York www.castlegarden.org

Catholic Family History Society www.catholic-history.org.uk/cfhs

The Catholic National Library www.catholic-library.org.uk/registers

The Catholic Record Society www.catholic-history.org.uk

The Commonwealth War Graves Commission
www.cwgc.org

Crew Lists (Merchant Shipping) www.crewlist.org.uk

Cyndi's List www.cyndislist.com

Dade Registers Article www.pontefractfhs.org.uk

Deceased Online www.deceasedonline.com

DirectGov (government access website)
www.direct.gov.uk

Documents Online
www.nationalarchives.gov.uk/documentsonline

Dr Williams's Library www.dwlib.co.uk [for the 'Dr
Williams's Library registers go to
www.nationalarchives.gov.uk]

Ellis Island, New York www.ellisisland.org

Familyrelatives www.familyrelatives.com

Familysearch www.familysearch.org

Federation of Family History Societies (contact details
for family history societies) www.ffhs.org.uk

Findmypast www.findmypast.co.uk

FreeBMD www.freebmd.org.uk

FreeCEN www.freecen.org.uk

Freepages
http://freepages.genealogy.rootsweb.ancestrey
.com/~hughwallis/IGIBatchNumbers

FreeREG www.freereg.org.uk

Gazettes Online www.gazettes-online.co.uk

Genes Reunited www.genesreunited.com

The Genealogist www.thegenealogist.co.uk

GENfair www.genfair.co.uk

GENUKI www.genuki.org.uk

General Register Office Certificate Ordering Service
www.direct.gov.uk/gro or
http://www.gro.gov.uk/gro/content/certificates/

Gentleman's Magazine 1731 to 1750
www.rsl.ox.ac.uk/ilej

The Guild of One-Name Studies www.one-name.org

Historical Directories www.historicaldirectories.org